1 MONTH OF
FREE
READING

at

www.ForgottenBooks.com

By purchasing this book you are eligible for one month membership to ForgottenBooks.com, giving you unlimited access to our entire collection of over 700,000 titles via our web site and mobile apps.

To claim your free month visit:

www.forgottenbooks.com/free688176

ISBN 978-0-484-43553-6
PIBN 10688176

AN EXAMINATION AND CORRECTION

OF

THE REPORT AND OPINION

OF

ATTORNEY GENERAL CLIFFORD TO THE PRESIDENT,

ON THE

SPANISH GRANTS FOR LANDS IN LOUISIANA,

KNOWN AS

THE HOUMAS CLAIM.

A report and opinion of the Attorney General, Nathan Clifford, to the President of the United States, appears in print, hearing date 31st December, 1847, and concluding—I. "That the grant to Maurice Conway is a complete and perfect Spanish grant to the extent of forty-two arpens from the river, and no more. That the said grant does not convey any lands beyond that extent, but that the title to the same is vested in the United States. II. That the patents which have been issued in the case of the Donaldson and Scott claim, and the Clark claim, were so issued without authority of law, and are therefore void and of no effect."

Upon this opinion and report the President has acted, so that judicial proceedings are ordered to be instituted to have the claims of the United States to the lands in the rear of the forty-two arpens in depth judicially determined.

Before such a step should have been taken on behalf of the Government, as an official act ordered by the President, three considerations should have been well weighed:

1st. The regard due to the faith of the United States, pledged by the law of nations, and by an express stipulation of the treaty by which they acquired Louisiana, that the inhabitants "shall be maintained and protected in the free enjoyment of their property;"

2d. The duty of the constituted authorities growing out of the very nature and purpose of government to abstain from harassing citizens by unfounded claims, vexatious litigations, and slander of their titles;

J. & G. S. Gideon, Printers.

3d. The probable event of success or defeat of the Government in the litigation proposed in the name of the United States, as actor, against persons claiming and holding lands under a Spanish-petition, concession, and possession, delivered in 1776, followed by a complete grant in 1777, upon its face, and words contradicting the limited extent assigned to it by Attorney General Clifford; claimed and held by the grantee and his assigns, as it is now claimed and held, during twenty-seven years succeeding the grant, before the territory was delivered to the United States; so claimed and held ever since; so claimed before the Commissioners appointed by the United States to hear and decide upon the validity of French and Spanish grants in Louisiana, and decided in favor of the claimants, in the year 1806, by the Commissioners as good and valid to the whole extent claimed; by them certified as good and valid, and laid before the Congress of the United States in 1812; and confirmed in 1814 by the Congress.

The Attorney General Clifford has perverted the meaning and effect of the Spanish grant to Maurice Conway, by misconception of the system of Spain in granting the lands in the provinces belonging to the Crown, by substituting his own notion of the rules of the English common law in place of the Spanish laws, usages, and customs, and by misjudging the powers and authorities of Spanish officers.

He has not duly considered, nor given due weight and respect, to the extensive sense and meaning given to this grant by the constituted authorities of Spain, and the possession given by those authorities, and continually held by the grantee and those claiming from and under him, according to such extensive sense and meaning of the grant during the Spanish dominion, and at the time Louisiana was ceded to the United States, and the change of national flags in 1803, constituting evidences of private rights held and enjoyed for upwards of twenty-seven years before the United States were possessed of the sovereignty, public domain, and jurisdiction of the Territory of Louisiana.

The Attorney General Clifford has not duly considered nor weighed the effect of the extensive sense allowed and confirmed under the Government of the United States; constituting, now, evidence of private right and enjoyment of more than seventy years of non-claim, either by the Government of Spain, or of France, or of the United States, during all that time.

He has not considered nor weighed the stain upon the public faith which may be the consequence of a proceeding by the Government of the United States now instituted to disturb a private right of such great antiquity, so begun and held, and enjoyed, under a foreign Government, and so continued for such a great length of time under the Government of the U. States.

The Attorney General Clifford has not discussed, nor duly weighed, the difference between a plea of length of time, by way of a positive bar prescribed by a statute of limitations, from which the Government may escape by the prerogative rule—nullum tempus occurrit regi; and length of time, used by way of evidence. From the presumption, founded on length of time and enjoyment, the Government cannot escape. The Crown, the Government, is bound by evidence—whether that evidence be positive or presumptive, direct or circumstantial.

The circumstances preceding and succeeding, and the expressions of the Spanish grant of 1776—1777 to Maurice Conway, as an addition to his former possession by grant of 1774, which addition the opinion of Attorney Genl. Clifford supposes to be only two arpens in depth, are so contradictory to such narrow interpretation, that, if duly weighed, the Executive ought to have foreseen defeat in a process of law instituted on behalf of the United States to enforce a construction so contracted and diminutive.

The virtues and vices of men in power are felt by the people. In the words of Ecclesiasticus: "A wise judge shall judge his people, and the " Government of a prudent man shall be steady.

" As the judge of the people is himself, so also are his ministers: " And what manner of man the ruler of a city is, such also are they that " dwell therein.

" An unwise king shall be the ruin of his people: and cities " shall be inhabited through the prudence of the rulers."

As the erroneous and indigested opinion of the Attorney General, reported by him to the President, has been the cause of an order from the Executive department of the Government, under the sanction of the President, to institute judicial proceedings to claim title for the United States to all the lands in the rear of the forty-two arpens in depth, by ninety-six arpens in front, and as this opinion has been printed with intent to circulate copies, I purpose to examine that opinion, demonstrate its errors, and prevent (as far as may be by freely combating those errors) the public mind from being abused by the erroneous opinion of the high law officer of the Executive department of the Government of the United States.

The errors may be comprised under three general heads—

1st. His erroneous construction of the Spanish grant to Maurice Conway upon his petition, the concession of Gov'r Gen'l Onzaga in 1776, the survey thereby made by Capt. Andry, the person specially appointed for that purpose, and the final complete grant thereon by Gov'r General Galvez in 1777. This erroneous construction is compounded of the Atto. Genl. Clifford's misconceptions of the laws, customs, and usages of Spain; of the powers, authorities, and duties of the Spanish officers; of the law of nations, and the treaty ceding Louisiana to the United States, as applied by him to this case.

2d. His erroneous construction of the acts of Congress.

3d. His neglect of the presumptive evidence in favor of the right of the possessors, because of the great length of time.

I. *The construction of the Spanish grant of* 1776 –'7.

To avoid confusion, and to bring the opinion of the Attorney Genl. Clifford to the proper test, it is to be observed, that whilst France held the dominion and possession of Louisiana, and before the cession to

Spain, a grant was made by France of a tract of land on the river Mississippi to the Bayou Goula and Houmas Indians; which land Maurice Conway and Alexander Latil purchased of the Indians in 1773, being forty arpens in depth, by ninety-six arpens in front, on the Mississippi river, as surveyed in 1773, and confirmed to Conway and Latil in 1774 by Onzaga, then the Spanish governor general of Louisiana.

Maurice Conway, having purchased Latil's moiety by deed of January 4, 1776, became sole possessor of this former tract of land of forty arpens in depth by ninety-six arpens front, originally granted by France to the Indians, purchased of the Indians by Conway and Latil, and assented to and confirmed by Ouzaga's grant of 1774.

Being so possessed, Conway petitioned for a grant, additional of all the vacant land in the rear, which was conceded by Onzaga, governor general, in 1776, and finally granted to Conway, in 1777, by Governor General Galvez.

Upon this additional grant the question arises; and Attorney General Clifford, by his construction, confines this addition to two arpens in depth.

The petition of Conway was made to Onzaga, bearing date 27th September, 1776, wherein he set forth, "that, being about to settle myself on the lands which Alexander Latil and I purchased with your approbation of the Houma Indians, and which are totally destitute of fences, and is cleared, for upwards of one league in depth, in such a manner that the cypress trees may be about one league and a half from the river, without my having any right to them, your excellency having granted to us only the depth of forty arpens, with which shortness of depth I cannot have access to the cypress trees, so necessary for the construction of my fences and other utilities of a plantation; therefore I humbly pray your excellency to take the circumstances into consideration, and to grant me all the depth which may be vacant behind or at the end of the aforesaid forty arpens of depth, whereof I am at present sole owner, by virtue of a deed of conveyance passed before Andrew Almonester, notary public, on the 4th January last, of the moiety belonging to Mr. Latil aforesaid. I pray your excellency to appoint Louis Andry to put me in possession of the aforesaid front and depth by fixing the needful boundaries, and furnishing me with due copies of the whole for my use and guide."

Upon this petition it is to be remarked, that Conway represented the lands to be cleared "in such a manner," for upwards of one league in depth, (not his own lands alone so cleared, for his depth of forty arpens was but the third of a league, but his own and the adjoining lands cleared for one league in depth,) as that the cypress trees were distant from the river about a league and a half; so that, on the face of the petition, Onzaga was asked to grant lands to include cypress trees distant one league and a half (or four and a half miles) from the river.

On this petition Onzaga made his decree and order, dated at New Orleans, 27th September, 1776, whereby he directed "Louis Andry, second adjutant of this place, to go to the land alluded to in the within memorial, and give the petitioner possession of that which may be vacant after the forty arpens in depth, of "which he is in possession, following the same directions, provided it be vacant, and that no injury is thereby done to any of the adjoining inhabitants; to which effect he shall establish his boundaries and limits, and of the whole proceedings he shall make a process verbal, of which he will make a return to us, signed by himself and the parties, in order to issue a complete title in due form to the claimant."

In obedience to that petition and decree, L. Andry, captain of infantry, and second adjutant and major of the city of New Orleans, reported that, on the first day of October, 1776, he went on the said land, "situated in the district of the parish of the Ascension or Lafourche, on the left bank of the Mississippi, about 22 leagues above the city of New Orleans, accompanied by the petitioner, Maurice Conway, and Louis Judice, commandant of said district," who sent for Calabe, chief of the Houma Indians, seller of the lands, "in order that he might point out the boundaries which are to limit the same on the upper and the lower sides;" which being done, he ascertained that (owing to intermediary changes of the adjacent owners) the lands now extended from the lower line of Francis Duhon, on the upper side, to that of Michael Chiasson, on the lower, which he measured, and found the old grant "contains ninety-six arpens in front on the river, opening one hundred and twenty degrees towards its rear, owing to its situation in the bottom of the bend; the upper line adjoining the lands of Francis Duhon, being directed north fifty degrees west; and the lower, adjoining those of Michael Chiasson, running north seventy degrees east; which lines are described in the figurative plat of my operations which I delivered to the party."

"The measurements of the front being concluded, I proceeded to put the petitioner in possession of the depth which by the aforesaid decree has been granted to him. To this end, having transferred myself to the upper line which joins Francis Duhon aforesaid, I examined in his presence the stakes which had been planted by me on the 22d December, 1773, which stakes still exist in the same situation, distance, and direction, both of mulberry tree; the first measuring five feet," &c., "planted at thirty-seven toises and two feet from the present margin of the river, and the second of six feet," &c., "planted at one arpent or thirty toises farther back towards the rear. Afterwards I proceeded on the same course, viz., north 50° west, until forty arpens in depth, opening for that purpose a road through the woods; at which point I caused to be planted a stake of cypress of six feet in length, &c.; and at two arpens farther still, that is at forty-two arpens from the river, I planted another stake, similar," &c.

"This line being drawn, I went to the lower one, common with Michael Chiasson, whom I also called, &c. I caused two stakes of mulberry wood to be planted on this line; the first at twenty toises from the present margin of the river, and the second at twenty toises farther back; in the aforesaid direction of north 70° east, on same line, at forty arpens in depth, I caused to be planted a cypress stake, and at two arpens farther still, (that is at 42 arpens from the river,) I caused to be planted another stake, of the same size of the precedent, in order to keep the course," (or, as another translator has it, in order that the direction may not deviate.)

"And to the end that all the above stated may be proven, I give the present certificate, signed by me, together with the party, Maurice Conway and the commandant aforesaid, and interpreter in this case—the chief of the Indians having declared, as well as the two adjoining neighbors, that they did not know how to sign; which I do attest," &c. Signed by Louis Andry, Maurice Conway, and Louis Judice.

On the 21st June, 1777, Bernardo de Galvez, then governor and intendant general of the province of Louisiana, having reference to the petition and proceedings of Andry, "relative to the possession given to Maurice Conway, pursuant to the above decree issued by my predecessor, of all the vacant land lying behind and on the rear of the first forty arpens which he possesses, by ninety-six arpens in front on the river, following the same direction of these; and finding them conformable to the rules of survey, and agreeable to the concessions of the adjoining inhabitants, without causing these last any harm or injury whatsoever, nor having by them been claimed, but on the contrary consented to it, as appears by their assistance to said operations—approving of the same, as we do by these presents approve, using of the power to us conferred by the King, we hereby do grant, in his royal name, to the said Maurice Conway the aforesaid land behind or at the end (or in the rear) of the forty arpens which contains his plantation, situated in the district of Lafourche, by ninety-six arpens in front on the river, following the same direction which those run, in order that, being his property, he may share and dispose of the same," &c.

The original title papers quoted were in the Spanish language. I have quoted from the translation made for the use of Mr. Gallatin when Secretary of the Treasury, and published in the first volume of the Laws of the United States, by Bioren, Duane & Weightman, arranged and printed, in the year 1815, under the authority of an act of Congress.

These title papers will be seen in that volume, (from page 551 to 554,) wherein the grant is noted as extending from the Mississippi to Lake Maurepas and the Iberville or Amite, and along the Amite, Iberville, and said lake.

The grant extends to all the vacant land behind and in the rear of the first forty arpens in depth by ninety-six arpens in front, as described by the fixed monuments and adjacent owners at the upper and the lower corners on the river Mississippi, with the courses of each line running off from the river given by degrees of the surveyor's compass, but marked and fixed on the ground, so that the courses may be invariably known and found.

The call for "vacant lands" is but *expressio eorum quæ tacite insunt,* and cannot hurt. Vacant land means land not before appropriated by private right—lands not severed from the public domain of the Crown—words inserted, ex abundante cautela, for the honor of the

Crown and certain information of his subjects. The grant to Conway, for all the vacant land within the boundaries given, is precisely the same in effect as if the words "vacant land" were substituted by the words "public land," or as if the words had been omitted. In cases of grants by the Government, public land is understood; "vacant land" is necessarily implied. The King could not grant that which was not his to grant, but the property of another.

If the lands within the specified courses from the Mississippi had in part been previously appropriated, then the quantity granted to Conway would have been lessened by so much; and it would have been as absurd to claim, under that grant, lands previously granted to other persons, as to have claimed to run across the Amite into the lands of a foreign province, not claimed by the Crown of Spain, but owned and possessed then by the Crown of Great Britain.

If the lands within the given courses, in the rear and on the back of the former grant, were not vacant at the date of the royal grant made by Galvez to Conway, what claim has the United States to those lands?

The recital in the grant of the possession given to Conway is "of all the vacant land lying behind and in the rear of the first forty arpens, which he possesses, by ninety-six arpens in front on the river, following the same direction as these;" the grant itself is for "the aforesaid land behind or at the end of the forty arpens which contains his plantation, situated in the district of Lafourche, by ninety-six in front on the river, following the same direction which those run." How far following the same direction which those run? The answer is, as far as the district of Lafourche extends. Within that boundary lands appropriated previously by private rights (if any such shall be found) are excepted necessarily, and by the grant of vacant lands, but taking in all vacant lands which the King may lawfully grant within the given lines and directions.

It must be presumed that the governors general, Onzaga and Galvez, knew the boundary of the district of Lafourche, and of the province of Louisiana, to which those lines would lead, by "following the same direction which those run;" and, so knowing, granted to Maurice Conway by those limits to take in all the vacant land which the King could lawfully grant. They knew that those lines, "following in the same direction," would extend to the natural boundary between the province of Louisiana, then possessed by Spain, and the province of West Florida, then possessed by Great Britain, and therefore granted by lines running in a direction which must be terminated by the boundary of the district of Lafourche, and which could not injure any subject, or other private right previously acquired.

The persons deriving titles under this grant sold and conveyed, held and possessed, during the Spanish sovereignty, claiming that the grant extended from the Mississippi, in depth, as far as could be found vacant, to the Amite, Iberville, or Lake Maurepas, (different names for the same stream.) The Spanish authorities so construed it, and sold the right of one of the sub-purchasers under Maurice Conway for public dues. The public authorities assessed, advertised, sold, and conveyed, in 1798, to the highest bidder, the land as extending from the Mississippi in depth, indefinitely, as far as not appropriated prior to the grant to Maurice Conway.

The notorious acts of assertion of title to the river Amite, by virtue of this grant, during the whole time of the Spanish sovereignty succeeding this grant, are numerous; the Attorney General makes an abstract of many of them, showing that the depth ran for vacant land.

The commissioners confirmed this claim under their grant as extending from the river Mississippi to the Amite.

The Attorney General makes the grant to stop at forty-two arpens in depth, so as to give to M. Conway, by the grant of 1776 and 1777, only two additional arpens in depth. This narrow riband the Attorney General has woven in the loom made by O'Reilly for the use of his subordinates; being of opinion that Governor General Galvez, (one of the successors of Governor General O'Reilly,) was bound to have wrought with the harness which O'Reilly had fixed for his subordinates, although Governor General O'Reilly was not bound by them himself.

Attorney General Clifford understands (or conceits he does) the Spanish laws, usages, customs, and ordinances, and the powers and authorities conferred by the King on his governors and intendants of the province of Louisiana, much better than the Spanish governors, Onzaga and Galvez, did. When the Spanish governor, Onzaga, has acted officially; when Andry has acted officially, and reported his official acts to Governor General Galvez; and when Governor Galvez, referring to the grant by his predecessor of all the vacant land, has approved the proceedings of Onzaga and Andry, and declared that he had found the proceedings "to be conformable to the rules of survey, and agreeable to the concessions of the adjoining inhabitants," &c., and therefore approved them; "and using of the faculty to us conferred by the King, do grant in his royal name to Maurice Conway the aforesaid land, behind or at the end of the forty arpens which contains his plantation, situated in the district of La Fourche, by ninety-six arpens in front on the river, following the same direction which those run;" the Attorney General Clifford harps upon the regulations made by O'Reilly, and argues upon them as having an effect to control, cut short, and wrest from their plain meaning the words and common sense of the petition, the decree of Onzaga, the operations of Andry, and the final complete grant of the Governor General Galvez. The Attorney General Clifford thinks that Galvez, in subserviency to the regulations made by O'Reilly, ought to have limited the grant to the depth of the two additional arpens, according to the two stakes set up by Andry at forty-two arpens from the river; that Governor General Galvez did wrong in approving the grant of *all* the vacant land in the rear, as made by Onzaga; did wrong in approving Andry's acts in putting Conway in possession of *all* the vacant land in the rear, and in not running and marking the back line to define the depth; did wrong in planting stakes to designate the continuing direction, so that it might not deviate; that Galvez did wrong in not stopping the grant at the end of forty-two arpens, and in granting *all* the vacant land at the end of the forty arpens, by ninety in front, "following the same direction as those run " So, sitting in judgment upon the official acts of the high officers of Spain, the Attorney General has in effect determined that they did not understand their powers, authorities, and duties; that they ought to have squared their official acts by the regulations of O'Reilly; and therefore perverts and distorts the words of the grant to a meaning and effect directly and palpably contradictory to the grant, in order to make it conform to O'Reilly's regulations.

Now it had come to pass, before the Attorney General wrote his opinion upon the matter of O'Reilly's regulations, that the Supreme Court of the United States had, upon solemn arguments, considered that same matter, and by repeated decisions had settled and established principles, to which the opinion of the Attorney General Clifford is in direct contradiction and disrespect.

The case of Delassus vs. United States, decided January term, 1835, 9 Peters, 132, 134, 135, was upon a grant made by Trudeau, lieutenant governor of the province of upper Louisiana, in pursuance of an official instruction to him by the governor general of the province of Lonisiana, the Baron de Carondelet, of the 1st April, 1795, of a tract of land containing a lead mine. The title under the concession had not been completed by a final grant before the cession of the province of Louisiana. The case was argued, on the part of the United States, by Attorney General Butler, who contended that this was an inchoate right, never confirmed by the governor general, a concession which Trudeau had no right to make, and that it did not conform to the regulations of O'Reilly made in 1770, confirmed by a royal order of the King of Spain.

The opinion of the Supreme Court was delivered by Chief Justice Marshall, in which, after commenting upon the first, second, and third articles of the treaty, he proceeds to say:

"A grant or concession made by that officer, who is by law authorized to make it, carries with it prima facie evidence that it is within his power. No excess or departure from them is to be presumed."

"This subject was fully discussed in the United States vs. Arredondo, 6 Peters, 691; Percheman vs. the United States, 7 Peters, 51; and the United States vs. Clarke, 8 Peters, 436. It is unnecessary to repeat the arguments contained in the opinions given by the court in those cases."

"The objection made to this plain title is, that the concession is not made in pursuance of the regulations of O'Reilly."

"This objection was considered in the cases heretofore decided by this court, and especially in 8 Peters, 455. It is apparent that those regulations were intended for the general government of subordinate officers; not to control and limit the powers of the person from whose will they emanated. The Baron de Carondelet, we must suppose, had all the powers which had been vested in Don O'Reilly. Had Governor O'Reilly made such a grant, could it have been alleged that he had disabled himself, by his instructions for the regulation of his subordi-

2

nate officers, from exercising the powers vested in him by the Crown; instructions which the power that created must have been capable of varying or annulling?''

In Arredondo's case, above referred to by the court, in answer to the objection that, in granting the quantity of 289,645 acres of land, the Spanish intendant had exceeded his authority, the Supreme Court said, ''the disposition of the royal domain was within the jurisdiction of the intendant; he had the power to make the grant, the terms and extent of which were within his discretion, of the proper exercise of which *this court* has neither the *power* nor the *right to judge.*

'' We will, however, observe, that we are well satisfied that the local authority was competent to make grants of lands of a greater quantity than that to which the *counsel* for the United States have contended they were limited; the United States have never insisted on limiting grants to such a pittance.'' (6 Peters, 746.)

These decisions of the Supreme Court of the United States utterly demolish the positions of Attorney General Clifford, of sitting in judgment upon the manner and extent of the exercise of powers by Onzaga and Galvez, in making the grant to M. Conway, and of reducing it to a pittance, by applying O'Reilly's regulations as a test.

Other cases have been subsequently decided by the Supreme Court of the United States in accordance with those principles, which will be noticed in examining another part of the opinion of the Attorney General.

O'Reilly's regulations, made to instruct his subordinates, have nothing to do with the construction of the concession of Governor General Onzaga, nor of the final grant of Governor General Galvez to Maurice Conway. Those regulations cannot subdue nor bend the words of the grant to Maurice Conway from their proper import and obvious meaning.

If these decisions of the Supreme Court had not been cited to the attention of the Attorney General Clifford, his argument insisting to bind the Governors General Onzaga and Galvez to the letter of O'Reilly's regulations for subordinates, might have been viewed with more toleration and patience, for want of the sciENTER; although the Attorney General of the United States was bound to have taken notice of those decisions in the absence of a special citation. But, as they were cited in an argument laid before him we may justly exclaim *Quousque* tandem, *abutere* Cliffordina, patientia nostra?

The idea that a grant for land cannot extend farther than the surveyor walked, or marked, however descriptive the certificate of survey and grant may be of a larger extent, is contrary to reason and practice.

Thousands and tens of thousands of acres of land have been adjudged to claimants in the courts, State and Federal, upon descriptions in grants purporting to be founded upon actual surveys of lands, upon which the surveyors never made, nor caused to be made, a corner, line, or mark, never stretched a chain, or put a foot, but sat in a chimney corner, and wrote certificates of survey, calling for corner trees never seen nor to be found, for lines never run nor marked; yet the certificates of survey and giants contained descriptions by which the lands could be ascertained, marked, and located. Successions of surveys and grants calling to adjoin, one after another, in a long chain, all depending upon the first link in the chain, have been established as good and valid, because the first had a certain fixed beginning, from which that and the dependant consecutive grants could be surveyed and identified. These grants were founded upon a statute requiring all surveyors, in making surveys, "to see the same plainly bounded by natural boundaries or marked trees."—(Old body of Virginia laws, 1748, chap. xiv, sect. vi, p. 220; Revised Code of Virginia of 1792, p. 152.)

Courts proceeded upon the maxim, "Id certum est, quod certum, reddi potest:" moreover, that it would be unjust that a person should lose his right by the mistake or neglect of a public officer over whose official acts he had no control.

In the Supreme Court of the United States various tracts of land have been adjudged to claimants upon the maxim "that is certain which can be rendered certain," by the descriptions alluded to in the grants; of which examples will be given hereafter.

The Attorney General has labored to control the grant by O'Reilly's regulations, and to make the depth only to the two stakes, on the one line and the other, set by Capt. Andry at forty-two arpens from the river, and to make the back line run from one of these stakes to the other, although Andry never run such a line, nor proposed such a boundary, in his written report of his proceedings, signed by him and by Judice and Conway, and delivered to Governor General Galvez. Andry ran from the upper corner on the river the line of the survey of 1773 and old grant of 1774, with the line of Duhon, No. 50 west, forty arpens, and planted a stake; he ran two arpens further on that course, and planted a stake; then he went to the lower corner of the old grant on the river, and from that he ran with the line of Chiasson, north 70° east, forty arpens, there planted a stake; at two arpens farther on the same line he planted a stake, "in order to keep the course."—(See vol. 1, Laws United States, by Bioren, p. 553.) To say that Andry, by this, intended the survey to run from this last stake to the stake on the upper line, is contrary to common sense.

The Attorney General says (p. 32) that, supposing the grant is not to be bounded by such a line from stake to stake, making the whole depth of the old and new grant only forty-two arpens, the grant "would be void for uncertainty."

In this, the opinion of the Attorney General runs counter to the decisions of the Supreme Court of the United States in these cases, (and others mentioned in these) : United States vs. Sibbald; 10 Peters, 313, 321. United States vs. Arredondo; 13 Peters, 133. United States vs. Low; 16 Peters, 162. United States vs. Clarke's heirs and Atkinson's heirs; 16 Peters, 231.

Sibbald's case arose out of a petition to the Spanish governor " for permission to build a water saw-mill on Little Trout and Nassau creeks, emptying into the river St. John on the north side, with a grant of land embraced in a line of two and a half miles to each wind, making a square of five miles, or its equivalent, in the event this situation will not permit the same form; which land is for a continual supply of timber." The Spanish governor made his decree or order granting the permission asked, "upon condition that, until the mill is built, the grant of the land, as asked, shall be of no account; and that the land shall be taken without injury to third persons."

Of the lands, 10,000 acres were surveyed on Trout creek; there being no more vacant land there, 4,000 acres were surveyed at Mosquito, about 30 miles south from the former; and 2,000 acres at Bowleg's hammock, about 20 miles west of the first.

The mill, by various accidents, although begun, was not completed until June, 1829, long after the cession of Florida to the United States.

As to the forfeiture claimed for non-compliance with the condition in time, as subsequently commanded by the governor before the cession, the court said: "The evidence is clear in this case, and others decided, that there is no instance in which a grant has been revoked or annulled by the Spanish authorities for any cause; nor of a Spanish governor having granted land which had been before granted on a condition; and it may well be doubted whether it would have been reannexed to the royal domain if the province had remained under the dominion of the King of Spain. Nor is there any provision of any law of Congress which specially requires the court to inquire into the performance of conditions on which grants were made." "The petitioner began the mill in time to save the forfeiture, and has shown a performance of such acts as amounts to a compliance with the condition, according to the rules of equity which govern these cases."

"It is in full proof, that the land could not be surveyed at the place designated without interfering with lands previously granted, which would have been contrary to the express words of the grant—without injury to third persons." "It was the *intention of the petitioner* and the *governor*, that there should be a grant of five miles square—"the equivalent for any deficiency on Trout creek may be referred to quantity rather than to the form of the survey." "The surveyor general testified it was an inherent privilege of a grantee to survey any land, which was designated by the grantee, to which no objection was made, so as to fill the grant without any order from the government. Such had been the practice as to vacant lands without any objection by any of the Spanish authorities. We are therefore of opinion, that the title to the whole quantity of land specified in the grant is valid, by the law of nations, of Spain, the United States, and the stipulations of the treaty for the cession of Florida; and ought to be confirmed to him according to the three surveys as made and returned with the record." Decree of confirmation; and that the surveyor of lands in the eastern district of Florida be enjoined to do, and cause to be done, all things, &c.

In the case of Arredondo's heirs, (13 Peters, 133,) the Spanish concession was made to F. Arredondo, 24th March, 1817, for 38,000 acres, "without prejudice to a third party, situate on the two banks of Alliga. tor creek, beginning about seven miles west of an Indian town called Alligator Town." The petitioner asked, inasmuch as the survey could not then be made, because the surveyor had other occupations, that the governor would be pleased to give him a grant which might, in the mean time, serve him as a title thereto. To which the governor respond. ed, "that the title corresponding will be issued to the petitioner as soon as he shall present the plot to be made by the surveyor; and, in the mean time, that this decree shall be an equivalent thereof in all its parts, of which a certificate shall be given to the petitioner, authenticated in due form, that the petitioner may prove said grant, and enjoy said lands, and dispose of them as he sees fit." No survey was made of the land whilst Florida continued subject to the Crown of Spain. "Nor does it appear that the survey has since been made, so as that the locality of the concession has since been definitely ascertained."

The Supreme Court said: "We do not consider the want of a survey as interfering with the right of the party to the land granted; but it must be taken, as near as may be, as it is described in the petition, where it was asked for, and as it was granted, and can not be taken elsewhere. If it can not be found there, the appellees have no claim to an equiva. lent. Or, if upon the survey it shall be found to interfere with previous grants to third parties, the concession will be lessened in quantity to the extent of the rights of third parties." Such are the terms of the con. cession, that the land is to be surveyed "in the place where the peti. tioner designates, without prejudice to a third party."

The decree confirmed the rights of the heirs of Arredondo, and gave directions for causing a survey, to give precise locality and identity to the land.

In the case of the United States *vs.* the Heirs of John Low, 16 Peters, 162, the petition was "for leave to build a saw-mill on Doctor's branch, and the grant of the accustomed quantity of land for the supply of lum. ber; permitting him to take 6.000 acres on Doctor's branch, and 10,000 acres on the northwest side of the head or lagoon of Indian river." The Spanish governor "grants him the permission he asked, likewise the land at the places he mentioned, upon condition that, until he erect. ed the said machine, he should not have an absolute right in the lands," &c.

The survey for six thousand acres was made on Doctor's branch 23d December, 1819; the survey for 10,000 acres was made 7th February, 1820, (after the cession of Florida to the United States,) northwestward. ly of the head of Indian river, and west of the prairies of North creek, which empties into the lagoon or head of Indian river. To this sur. vey, so made after the cession, the United States objected; and also ob. jected that the survey departed from "the head or lagoon of Indian riv. er, and did not touch it."

The Supreme Court said: "According to the strict ideas of conform. ing a survey to a location in the United States, the survey should have been made adjoining the natural object called for; and, therefore, the head of the lagoon would necessarily have formed one boundary. But it is obvious, more latitude was allowed in the province of Florida. The object of the grant was timbered land, fit for the supply of lumber; and if the nearest *vacant* timbered land to the head of the lagoon was surveyed, the *intentions* of the government and of the grantee were complied with." The decree of the court, made in favor of the claimants for both tracts of land, was affirmed.

In the case of United States *vs.* Clarke and others, 16 Peters, 231, George Atkinson had petitioned the Spanish governor, " in consideration of various important services and losses through a series of years, to grant him, in property, 15,000 acres of land in Cedar Swamp, and on the west of Upper Little lake. The governor granted the land in property—the surveyor general will run them for him in the places he mentions, or in others that are vacant and of equal convenience to the party." The lands were surveyed, on four places, in January and March, 1818; none of them at the places designated by the petition.

" By the 8th article of the Florida treaty, no *grants* made after the 24th January, 1818, were valid; nor could a survey be valid on lands other than those authorized by the grant. Still the power to *survey* existed up to the change of flags."

"That Spain had the power to make grants founded on any consideration, and subject to any restrictions within her discretion, is settled." "Imperfect titles were equally binding on this Government, after the cession, as they had been on the Government of Spain before: Arredondo's case, 6 Peters, 706. Percheman's case, 7 Peters, 51. The grant was to Atkinson for the lands he mentioned, or for any other lands that were vacant. The surveyor did not exceed the grant by going to other places than those pointed out in the petition." The decree of the court below, confirming the claimants of the land in the four surveys as made was affirmed.

These cases, decided by the Supreme Court of the United States, establish these principles:

1. That a Spanish grant for "vacant land" is not, by such expression, rendered void for uncertainty; those words only lessen the quantity if previous grants be found within the proposed boundaries.

2. That Spanish grants are to be taken and explained according to the usages and customs of Spain, and of the officers of that Government; and are not to be tested by the rigid rules and technicalities of the common law as used in the United States.

3. That all grants and concessions made by Spain, whilst Louisiana and Florida respectively were possessed by Spain, are equally binding upon the Government of the United States after the cession, as they had been on the Spanish government before the cession to the United States.

4. That those concessions, orders of survey, and grants, made by the constituted authorities of Spain, are to be expounded liberally, equitably, and according to the intentions of the petitioner and the grantor.

The justice, equity, and liberality of construction given to Spanish grants for the purpose of preserving the faith of the treaties of cession, and observing the laws, usages, and customs of Spain, and the law of nations, present a striking contrast and signal rebuke to that spirit of rigor, narrowness, and covetous desire to cut short the Spanish grant displayed by Attorney General Clifford in his opinion.

The expressions "vacant land," "public land," "without prejudice to a third party," all convey the same idea in the royal concessions, orders of survey, and grants. Previous appropriations are necessarily exceptions out of the grants for the lands of the public domain. If the exception be not expressed, it is necessarily implied, as being of the essence and very nature of the contract.

In the treaty by which Louisiana was acquired by the United States, the words of the second article declares, "in the cession made by the preceding article are included the adjacent islands belonging to Louisiana. All public lots and squares, *vacant lands*, and all public buildings, fortifications, barracks, and other edifices, which are not private property."

Will Attorney General Clifford say that the words, "vacant lands," in that grant, or the words "public lots and squares," or the words "other edifices which are not private property," are not good words of purchase, void for uncertainty?

Will Attorney General Clifford pretend that the letters patent, and royal grants of the Kings of England, to various subjects, for territories in America, lying along the Atlantic coasts, between certain points, and extending westwardly by the designated parallels of latitude indefinitely, to include the parts and "territories in America, either appertaining unto us, or which are not now actually possessed by any Christian Prince or people," were all void for uncertainty, because there was no definite boundary back from the Atlantic coast, at which the runnings of the parallels of latitude were to stop, because the extent along the lines was depending upon the fact whether or not Christian princes, as for example, France, Spain, Russia, or Holland, had possession within the lines and directions so continued? The voices of princes, States, and potentates have answered, no. The extent of the territories was determined by ascertaining the fact, whether such previous rights and possessions existed, and to such the proprietary and colonial rights derived from the Crown of England had to yield. For all the residue, not in conflict with previous rights, the grants were good and valid.

The petition to Onzaga, and his order and concession upon the petition, alludes to the back of the old grant.

Andry could not execute his duty under the warrant to him without having ascertained the precise locality of the front upon the river Mississippi, and the courses of the lines from the river to the depth of forty arpens, comprising the land whereof Conway was the proprietor, as represented in the petition, and Ouzaga's order thereupon. When that was ascertained, Andry proceeded to put Conway into possession of all the vacant land in the rear, following the same direction by the lines from the river, which he had run and marked by stakes, to keep the courses, that they may not deviate.

Andry's warrant, duty, and office, was to put Conway "in possession of that which may be vacant after the forty arpens in depth, of which he is in possession, following the same directions." So was the petition, so was the concession and order upon the petition. His authority, duty, and power was to put Conway in possession of the back land, all the vacant land in the rear following the same courses, the same directions as the front land possessed by him. So much Andry did; he put Conway in possession of all the vacant land in the rear, by the directions ascertained and invariably fixed. The two stakes, one upon each line; two arpens farther in the rear, he set, not as corners, not to limit the depth, but "in order to keep the course." So Andry understood, so reported it, and so Galvez understood it, and so the governor general explains in the recital of Andry's survey and report, and in the words of the final grant made by the governor. The intention of the petitioner, the intention of Governor Onzaga, the intention of Andry, the surveyor, and the intention of Governor Galvez, of each and all, are concurrent, uniform, clear, and palpable to that effect, insomuch that no Spaniard ever doubted it during all the time from October, 1776, to the cession of Louisiana and the change of flags in 1803. The commissioners so understood it; the Congress so understood it.

It has happened, that about the close of the year 1847, and just before the coming in of the new year 1848, Attorney General Clifford has seen a new light, viz., that Onzaga and Galvez, the governors general of the Spanish province of Louisiana, did not understand the Spanish laws, customs, usages, and authorities under which they were acting; that the intendant general of the royal revenue of the province of Louisiana, and the commandant of the district of Lafourche, and Andry, and the Spanish subjects, and the commissioners appointed by the United States to ascertain and adjust the title to land in Louisiana, and the Congress of April, 1814, did not understand these matters; and that even the Supreme court of the United States, in various cases, have missed the longitude,

> Which he (more lucky than Will Whiston,
> Or that other good master Ditton,)
> Thinks he has so happily hit on.

The Attorney General Clifford makes, by his commentary on the petition of Conway, in 1776, the grant of Governor General Onzaga thereupon, the report of Andry, in obedience to the order to him from Onzaga, and the grant of the Governor General Galvez upon these in 1777, to amount to nothing but an additional grant of two arpens in depth, beyond the old depth of which Conway was previously possessed, by virtue of the purchase of the Houmas and Bayagoula Indians, confirmed to Conway and Latil, by the governor, Onzaga, in 1774, and by Conway's purchase of Latil's moiety, by deed of 4th January, 1776.

The avowed purpose of the petition was for the vacant land in the rear of his possession, of forty arpens in depth by ninety-six arpens in front, upon the river Mississippi, for a supply of "cypress trees necessary for the construction of fences and other utilities of the plantation."

The petitioner stated that the cypress trees were "about one league and a half from the river," and by the shortness of depth of forty arpens he could not have access to them. The intent of the petitioner, and the intent of the grantor, Governor General Onzaga, was a grant of all the vacant land in the rear, so that the petitioner might have the cypress trees. Therefore it was necessarily understood by Onzaga that the petitioner intended the addition to run not less than one league and a half, measured from the river; otherwise he could not reach the cypress trees, which were at that distance.

An arpent consists of thirty toises, of six feet to each toise, of Paris measure, equal each toise to six feet six inches of English measure. The forty-two arpens, at which the Attorney General stops the grant, are only twelve hundred and sixty toises. One league and a half from the river to reach the cypress trees would require thirty-six hundred toises. So that the Attorney General would stop the grant twenty-three hundred and forty toises (about three miles of English measure) short of the cypress trees, so specially intended to be included in the concession of Onzaga. By this, the avowed purpose and intention of the petitioner and the grantor would be frustrated; the petitioner would get an addition to his former possession of a pittance of two arpens in depth, (equal to about one hundred and thirty-three and a third yards, or twenty-three perches of our measure,) not worth at that day the expense and trouble of the petition, survey, and grant.

This short addition of two arpens to the former shortness of forty arpens in depth, certainly cannot be the thing for which Conway petitioned; which Onzaga conceded; which Andry was ordered to do; for which Andry operated, by calling to his assistance the commandant, Judice, of the district of Lafourche, who sent for the Indian chief Calabe to show the former boundary, and called Duhon, who showed his boundary, and Chiasson, who showed his boundary; for which Andry measured and planted stakes to preserve the courses from deviation, made his figurative plan and sketch and written report to Galvez, and for which he made the final grant to Conway for all the vacant land in the rear of Conway's former possession of forty arpens in depth by ninety-six arpens in front, "following the same direction as these"—"following the same direction which those run."

This short, narrow, diminutive, ridiculous outcome never was suggested by the Spanish authorities or Spanish people during the time the country remained under the dominion of the crown of Spain; nor is it consistent with the proper construction of the petition, concession, survey, and final grant. It is the offspring of the laborious dissertations of Attorney General Clifford upon the laws, usages, and customs of Spain, O'Reilly's regulations, the law of nations, and the treaty, as seen in his report and opinion to the President. Like curious and prodigious issues from laborious throes, have happened before. It is said (and in print) that, once upon a time, a small mouse crept into the tube of a

3

telescope, and was by accident shut up in close restraint between two of the glasses, whereby to the vision of some literati, who looked through this telescope, gazing at the moon, the little mouse was magnified and mistaken for an elephant in the moon. Again, it has been written, and printed, that, as a mouse brought forth such a prodigy, a mighty mountain grew great with child, was in labor, and brought forth a ridiculous mouse.

Attorney General Clifford says, (p. 34,) " the recital which represents that the front had been cleared out upwards of a league needs confirmation, and cannot well be reconciled with the operations in the field, if it be admitted that the cypress constituted the principal growth, which does not appear to be denied. The surveyor found it necessary to cut a road through the woods, in order to run the course one half that distance, rendering it apparent that the petition had been prepared without any precise knowledge of distances, or of the actual state of things on the land.''

The proposed inquiries, to be solved by oral testimony after the lapse of upwards of seventy years—what kind of woods Andry cut through? Whether cypress timber trees or saplings of second growth, and of what species? How far he cut through, and what sized trees he cut, in running upon that upper line? Or how broad was the belt of woods he ran through on that line? Whether it was as broad as the riband of two arpens which the Attorney General assigns to Conway for the addition to his former possession? Or how much cypress timber for fences and other utilities of the plantation could have been obtained from the old grant, without the addition petitioned for? Or how far it was indispensably necessary to run, in addition to the former shortness of depth, so as to give a plentiful supply of cypress for fences and other utilities?—appear to be not pertinent at this day and time, after the complete and final grant made by Galvez for all the vacant land in the rear. If the governor general of Louisiana was content with the statements in the petition, and thereupon deemed it convenient to grant all the vacant land in the rear of the plantation to Conway, it is not perceived what right the United States have, who claim by the post-cession in 1803, to complain of the grant of Galvez of 1777, as having run farther than necessary to reach the cypress trees, and give sufficient supply of timber for fences and other utilities. This make-weight, which the Attorney General has so attempted to throw into the scale, appears thin as air, lighter than cork, and not worth a grain of mustard seed.

The petition, and concession, and direction to Andry, and final grant, had no limitation within the side lines other than previous private rights. All vacant and unappropriated lands falling within the given courses were included. To stop at an additional depth of two arpens (one hundred and twenty yards only) is manifestly contradictory to the intention of the petitioner and the Spanish officers—an outrage upon the meaning of the title papers.

The courses which Andry did run are reported distinctly by him— the one north 50° west, the other north 70° east; on which he set up,

and firmly planted in the ground, stakes "in order to keep the course."
So is his official certificate of what he did, and of his intent in so doing.

But now, at the close of the year 1847, when two generations have
passed, and many of the third generation also sleep in the grave, after
all the parties to the original transactions are dead, Attorney General
Clifford makes a commentary upon their acts and their intentions directly contrary to those intentions and declarations which they have
left behind them in official writings, as parts of the res gestæ, done in
solemn form. He supposes that Onzaga and Galvez misunderstood
their powers, authorities, and duties to their sovereign; that he understands them better than those high officers of the crown did; that the
grant of Galvez, instead of "following the same direction which those
run," which were particularly reported to him, shall run in a course and
manner not reported, not named—either by Andry, Onzaga, or Galvez—no where visible, nor described, nor proposed by Andry, and in
contradiction to the plain meaning and intent of the papers and writings
and solemn memorials of those days and times.

On the 5th March, 1778, Maurice Conway by deed, acknowledged
before the proper officer and recorded, sold and conveyed to O. Pollock
a part of this tract of land, fronting on the Mississippi thirty-six arpens,
and running back in depth " as far as the lake."

On the 5th February, 1795, William Conway, heir of Maurice Conway, mortgaged to William Pollock another part, thirty arpens in front,
"and depth as far as the lake."

April 7th, 1798, William Conway mortgaged to John Joyce thirty
arpens of "front and depth as far as the lake."

In 1798, the intendant general of the royal revenue, and the commandant of the district of Lafourche, caused a part of this tract belonging to the estate of Maxent, derived under said Conway's grant, assessed for the public dues for maintaining the levee or embankment, to
be valued, advertised, and sold, as fronting twenty-nine arpens on the
river, "by upwards of four leagues in depth." The appraisement was
ordered by Morales, intendant of the royal revenue, to be made as being
"in depth upwards of four leagues;" it was accordingly so appraised
by two appraisers called for the purpose, it was advertised 9th August,
1798, in the Gazette, as containing a front "by about four leagues in
depth." Evan Jones, the commandant of the district, sold it under
the appraisement; Louis Faure became the best bidder, offering more
than two-thirds of the appraised value; the commandant adjudged
Faure to be the buyer, and conveyed to him as purchaser at the sale,
describing the land as "measuring twenty-nine arpens in front, by
the depth which could be found."

Because the commandant of the district of Lafourche, Evan Jones,
in the title paper he gave the purchaser, Faure, did not pursue the precise description of depth mentioned in the order of appraisement, and in
the advertisement, but changed it to "the depth which could be found,"
Attorney General Clifford thinks that change "worthy of special notice,"
as not militating against his notion that the grant is limited to forty two

arpens in depth, from the Mississippi river. An order of the intendant general of the royal revenue, of 3d August, 1798, directed~~~~Simon Ducarneau and Alexo Lesassier, ("two persons named to him by Evan Jones, the commandant, as being two persons sufficiently acquainted with the quality and circumstances of the land,") to appraise the land. They did accordingly appraise it, "considering the said lands measure about twenty-nine arpens in front, by upwards of four leagues in depth," at the sum of twenty-four hundred dollars. The order of Morales upon that appraisement was made on the 3d August, 1798, directing the notary to call on the printer, "and showing him the aforegoing appraisement, cause him to publish a notice informing the public that the sale of the said land shall take place on the 13th inst., at 4 o'clock, at the intendant's house;" the printer did publish the notice in the Gazette of 9th August. On the 6th August, 1798, Morales entered his decree, declaring the sale at his house was intended only in case Evan Jones, commandant of Lafourche, should not have been able to sell the said land; therefore, "let an order to him issue, containing the appraisement and this decree, directing him (Evan Jones, commandant of Lafourche,) to proceed to the said sale for cash, provided the price bidden for it be upwards of the two-thirds of the appraised value, there being no higher bidder, to pay the sum due for the making of the levee, causing the receipt thereof to be annexed to the proceedings," and to give due notice before the thirteenth instant, conformably to what has been already decreed on this subject."

Evan Jones, the commandant, did sell under that appraisement, under the order to him of the 6th August, by Morales, containing the front and depth, and appraisement, and did sell for upwards of two-thirds of the appraised value, and sold and completed the sale to Faure, on the 12th August, 1798, so as to render the sale by Morales unnecessary, as expressed in his decree and order to Evan Jones to sell, made on 6th August, 1798, and communicated to the commandant.

As Morales declared the land was upwards of four leagues in depth, (upwards of twelve French miles,) caused it to be appraised as so extending, as the appraised value was set upon it as so extending, and was sold as so extending; these public official acts are evidences of the construction of the grant to Conway, are evidences to explain the meaning and sense of certain terms and words employed in the grant, as understood by the officers and people of Spain. Surely they do negative and contradict the construction of the Attorney General, Clifford, that it was limited and confined to the depth of forty-two arpens only from the river Mississippi; they explain that the grant does not stop at the depth of forty-two arpens, that it runs on upwards of four leagues; that it was a grant which, in its language and terms, runs on and includes, within the given courses, all the vacant land.

The final act of the commandant in giving the title to the purchaser, Faure, coincides with the construction of Morales in the valuation and the advertisement, declaring by the title paper delivered to Faure, that it entitles him to all the vacant land in the rear of his twenty-nine arpens in front, not even limiting it to a depth of four leagues, but conveying to him the land "as measuring twenty-nine arpens in front by the depth which could be found," meaning that could be there found not previously appropriated; even beyond the four leagues, if vacant, and in the district of Lafourche—not limited to a depth of forty-two arpens.

Those governmental proceedings are clear and unequivocal explanations of the meaning and sense of the grant to Conway, as understood by the officers and people of Spain of that day and place. It is an insult to common sense to say that the commandant, Evan Jones, intended by the title paper he gave to the best bidder and purchaser, Faure, to limit him to the depth of only forty-two arpens, within which to look for his rights, and for lands not previously granted by the King to persons other than Maurice Conway.

That all the land in the rear and on the back of the first grant of ninety-six arpens in front by forty arpens in depth, following in the same direction as those, was vacant when the second grant of 1776, 1777 was made to M. Conway, as far as to the most eastwardly and southwardly boundary of the district of Lafourche, is now well ascertained and evinced by the claim set up for the United States; for if it had been granted to others previously to the date of the grant to M. Conway, then it was not vacant and belonging to the public domain at the time of the cession to the United States, and they can have no title to it.

The expression, "by the depth which can be found," is an opposite, the very reverse to the limited boundary fixed by stakes, at the depth of forty-two arpens; independent of the import of the words themselves, the proceedings which led to the official sale, and the conveyance there under to Faure, explain the meaning which use had affixed to them in the language of the people of those days, and of the constituted authorities of that country.

In the Attorney General Clifford's printed opinion and report, pages 11 and 12, other conveyances between vendors and vendees are noted, dated in 1785, 1786. and 1802, before the cession to the United States, in which the expressions used as to depth are "depth which corresponds with the title granted by this government to Maurice Conway," "with the depth which comprehends the title of the said land," "with the depth according to the title of concesssion that his excellency, Señor Count Galvez, gave by his decree of 21 June, 1777;" all of which show that from the beginning this title was never bought or sold as limited to forty-two arpens in depth, but the reverse. Not a deed has been found limiting this grant to forty-two arpens in depth, before the cession of the country to the United States, or since. All the sales and purchases during the occupancy of the country by Spain show that the title granted to Conway was not limited to a depth of forty-two arpens, but for all the depth that was vacant and not previously appropriated. The claims were laid in before the commissioners by plats, showing the claims as extending to the Amité and Lake Maurepas, and the commissioners so allowed and confirmed them in 1806.

The maxim of law is, "contemporanea expositio est fortissima in lege." 2 Inst., 11, 136, 181.

The exposition by the constituted authorities and people of Spain, involving matters of their own day and time, their own language, idioms, laws, usages, customs, and tenures of property, deserves the highest respect from the constituted authorities of a different Government, of people of a different language, brought up under different laws, different usages, a different policy as to the disposal of the public domain, and different modes of speech to express the tenures of estates.

By the common law of England, which we inherited, the words "to him and his heirs" were required to convey a fee simple; without the word "heirs" the grant conveyed only an estate for the life of the grantee. No such words were necessary, by the Spanish laws, to grant and convey an estate in lands in absolute and perpetual property. In the grant to Maurice Conway, the word "heirs" is not inserted. If Attorney General Clifford, in applying his common law notions to this Spanish grant, had raised the objection that, for want of the words "to his heirs," Maurice Conway took only an estate for his life, which had dropped, such an objection would not have been a jot more ill founded than his objection to the Spanish expression, "all the vacant land lying behind, or in the rear, of the first forty arpens in depth, by ninety-six in front." Those expressions were as well understood by the French and Spanish people of Louisiana, when the country was possessed by Spain, as the words "to him and his heirs forever in fee simple," are understood by our people of the old thirteen United States.

To give color to the proposition, that if the grant be not stopped at forty-two arpens, it is void for uncertainty, the Attorney General has cited the cases in 3 Howard, 786; 15 Peters, 184, and 215, and 319; and 16 Peters, 159.

The case in 3 Howard, 773, 774, 785, 786, is that of the United States vs. King et al., in which the grant to the Marquis de Maison Rouge was held invalid. The decision is founded upon the determination that the "certificate of Trudeau is antedated and fraudulent;" that the survey and plat to which Trudeau's certificate, bearing date 14 June, 1798, is made to apply, "was not made in the lifetime of the Marquis de Maison Rouge, but after his death." This survey and plat being so swept away, (in the opinion of the court,) there was nothing whatever to give locality to the claim; for it will be seen by the concession to the Marquis by the Baron de Carondelet, that no locality whatever could be assigned to the claim, if the after survey, by which locality and identity was asserted, was taken away as fraudulent and antedated. This decision, however, (in principle not bearing upon the boundary of the Houmas claim,) the Supreme Court, at their present term, 1847, have had occasion to review, and have declared that the court in that decision and mandate at January term, 1845, committed a mistake, ran counter to principles correctly and firmly established by the antecedent decisions of the Supreme Court of the United States, and by an entry on their minutes have recommended to the Attorney General of the United States that the decree and mandate of January term, 1845, be set aside for the sake of justice.

The case in 15 Peters, 184, United States *vs*. Forbes, was upon Forbes' petition to abandon a former concession for 15,000 acres, because of his inability to comply with its terms, "and in lieu thereof to grant me an equivalent in the district of Nassau river of ten thousand acres." The Spanish governor, upon this petition, endorsed a permission to abandon the fifteen thousand acres, "and in lieu of them the ten thousand acres are granted to him without prejudice to a third party, for the objects solicited, in the *district* or bank of the river Nassau." There being nothing else whereby to locate this concession, the court decided the description entirely too vague and indefinite to attach it to any identical tract of land.

The case in 15 Peters, 215, the Widow and Heirs of Buyck *vs*. The United States, was upon a petition setting forth that Augustin Buyck "having a large number of negroes, and there being also some white persons, native citizens of the United States of America, who wish to join him for the settlement and cultivation of lands at Musquito, he solicits that this government will grant him fifty thousand acres south and north of said place, with the privilege of and asking for more in proper time, as he may need it." The Spanish governor endorsed "the land which the party solicits is granted to him in manner as he proposes, and with condition that he shall not cede any part thereof to any person whatever, without the knowledge and approbation of the Government." This description, not being aided by any after proceeding, the Court decided it too vague and uncertain to give identity or locality for any particular tract of land; Musquito inlet on the eastern coast of the peninsula, made by Halifax river or lagoon, extending from Musquito bar northward more than twenty miles, and by the southern or Hillsborough lagoon extending a distance of forty miles.

The case in 15 Peters, 275, 279, O'Hara *vs*. The United States, arose upon O'Hara's petition to the Spanish governor, stating that he intended to settle in the province, and asked that the governor would "grant fifteen thousand acres of land out of those vacant between the rivers St. John and St. Mary's, in the place called Nassau; and in case said vacant lands do not comprehend the number of acres he solicits, to grant him the deficiency on the river St. Mary's, and he obligates himself to take possession of the said lands within the term of six months."

The governor's decree stated, "the lands solicited by the petitioner are hereby granted to him in the place indicated, without prejudice to a third party, and until the time when, in conformity to the number of workers he may have to cultivate them, the corresponding number of acres may be surveyed to him." The court say, O'Hara "never made a settlement," "never took his family or negroes to the land." The decree restrained the right to the number of workers; the promulgated regulations declared the quantity for each worker, for the head of the family, for children, &c., &c., so that "there is no grant for any quantity; the grant itself was too indefinite to convey any land, unless a survey had been made, and had been recognised by the Spanish authorities, or unless the grantee had settled and occupied land under that decree, in which event a survey might have been presumed." Such a place called Nassau is not known, unless is meant by it all the land between Nassau river and the St. John's and St. Mary's; it is equidistant, or nearly so, from those, and wends its way to the Atlantic in a course of fifty or sixty miles. If the land is to be taken on the Nassau, where shall a survey be begun? And on what part of the St. Mary's shall the deficiency in quantity be taken, supposing a part can be found in the place called Nassau? The St. Mary's is known as the boundary between Florida and Georgia, and that its head or source is the Oquafanoche swamp; it is navigable for a hundred miles, &c. The grant is therefore void on account of uncertainty."

Not because it called for vacant land, but because it had no beginning, no specialty, but such an extensive range wherein to begin, and not any description "in such a way as to distinguish it from things of a like kind, nor has the identity of the grant been shown by extraneous evidence."

The case in 15 Peters, 319, The United States *vs.* Delespine, arose upon the petition of Arambide to the council of East Florida for "two leagues to each point of the compass, *to the north of the river Miamies.*" The court said (p. 334,) "that the land was to have been selected in the neighborhood of some part of the river, and north of it, is sufficiently plain; but whether near the ocean, or near what other part of the river, does not appear, and for an obvious reason, the grantee reserved to himself the right to produce the plat of the said lands as soon as he found himself prepared to take it out, and to commence the establishment he was to effect. This was never done, and no particular lands could have been decreed to Arambide, had the council at St. Augustine possessed the power to grant." "It was not possible for the superior court to locate any land, as no particular spot was granted; lands not previously granted were, by the treaty, vested in the United States as part of the public domain."

The case in 16 Peters, 153 to 161, The United States *vs.* Miranda and others, arose out of a petition of Miranda for a grant "of eight leagues in the royal lands, which are found on the waters of Hillsborough and Tampa bays, in this province." The Spanish governor's decree of 26th Nov., 1810, was, "I grant to him, in the terms which he solicits, the said quantity of land, to be laid off in the places which he indicates, without prejudice to a third party."

The court say, (p. 156,) "no survey of the land was made whilst Florida was a province of Spain, nor was any attempt made by the grantee, or by any agent, or any person claiming under him, to occupy any land under this grant, or to make a survey of it until after the Floridas had been ceded to the United States. The grant is void, no land having been severed from the public domain previous to the 24th Janu-

ary, 1818, and because the calls of the grant are to indefinite for locali.
ty to be given to them."

"Tampa, or Espiritu Santa, as it was known or called before Florida
was ceded to the United States, is at least forty miles long, and in one
or more places from thirty to forty miles broad. Hillsborough empties
into it from the north, &c., &c. The eastern part of this bay was called Hillsborough, and the little bay attached to the north side Tampa."
&c. "Where in this extensive area shall this grant be located?"
&c., &c.

" By grants of land we do not mean the mere grant itself, but the
right, title, legal possession, and estate, property and ownership, legally
resulting upon a grant of land to the owner. But in the case before
us, for want of a survey, or some point for the beginning of one, there
can be neither a seisin in fact or in law; for identity of premises is as
essential for a seisin in law as is necessarily implied in a seisin in fact.
The treaty imposes upon the United States no obligation to make a
title to lands of which the grantee had neither an actual seisin nor a
seisin in law. Identity is essential for the latter, and has uniformly
been in the contemplation of this court when it has confirmed Florida
grants inchoate or complete."

Such are the precedents cited by Attorney General Clifford as as-
similated to the grant made to Conway upon his petition; the concession by Onzaga, the survey by Andry, and final grant by Galvez, for
land designated, located, identified, and described, by reference to the
Mississippi river as a natural boundary in front, having its precise locality on that river fixed by monuments and abuttals, at the upper
corner and at the lower corner, measured from the one to the other at
ninety-six arpens, with given courses of the side lines running from the
river, the line from the upper corner joining Duhon, and running north
fifty degrees west; that from the lower corner joining Chiasson, and
running north seventy degrees east, each course made visible by stakes
firmly planted upon the lines, that the courses may be kept without
any deviation. The petition of M. Conway, the concession and decree of Governor Onzaga, the survey of Andry, and the final grant of
Governor Galvez, all concurring to give to Conway property and possession "of all the vacant lying behind and on the rear of the first
forty arpens which he possesses, by ninety-six arpens in front on the
river, which contain his plantation, situated in the district of Lafourche,
following the same direction which those run, in order that, it being his
property, he may share and dispose of the same."

This grant to Conway, so defined, located, fixed, and described,
by boundaries natural and artificial, and by given courses from the fixed
corners of adjoining proprietors, the Attorney General Clifford likens to
the petitions and grants without any survey, without any courses, without any place of beginning, without any specialty, and without any
description whereby to construct and mark out a locality.

In comparing things so unlike, and founding an argument upon such
supposititious likeness, that the additional grant of 1776 must be cut short

to the pittance of two arpens in depth beyond the grant of 1774, under the shallow pretension that a continuation of the same two certain courses to include the rear lands at a greater depth than forty-two arpens would make the grant void for uncertainty, Attorney General Clifford has displayed either a lack of the faculty of discrimination, or a misconception of his official station and duty.

On such an occasion, calling for his advice to the President upon a subject involving the private rights and interests of citizens, the public faith, the obligation of the law of nations, and the sacred faith of the treaty, an elegant propriety commanded the Attorney General of the United States to scorn the pettifogger, and perform the part of a candid circumspect counsellor, of a discreet firm jurisconsult.

The Attorney General Clifford admits and declares, that the lands described in the grant as bounded on the river Mississippi ninety-six arpens in front, between Duhon on the upper side and Chiasson on the lower side, and between the lines running off from the river, north fifty degrees west from the corner of Duhon, and north seventy degrees east from the corner of Chiasson on the river, and so opening from the river, are certainly located and defined to the extent of forty-two arpens, measured on each line from the river. How, then, can there be any uncertainty and insufficiency of description and locality of the lands in the rear, contained within the same two certain courses continued on from the distance of forty-two arpens, "following the same direction which those run," onward to the boundary of the district of Lafourche, at the river Amite, Iberville, and Lake Maurepas?

The propositions, the one that the first forty arpens in depth, by ninety-six arpens in front, included within the two side lines from the river Mississippi, north fifty degrees west from the upper corner, and north seventy degrees east from the lower corner on the river, extended to the distance of forty arpens on each course, are lands certainly described, and well located and defined; the other, that the lands included within the same lines continued, lying on the back and in the rear of the first forty arpens in depth, by ninety-six arpens in front, "following the same direction which those run" to the Amite, are not specially described, not well defined, but that the grant for the continuation of those same lines shall be void for uncertainty, are inconsistent propositions. The argument that the lands to the extent of forty-two arpens in depth between those given lines are certain, but that the lands in the rear thereof, if those same lines be continued, become uncertain, vague, and insufficiently described by the grant, is absurd.

Both descriptions of the lands contained within the lines given extending from the Mississippi river, as well the first forty arpens in depth as the after lands in rear between the same lines continued to the boundary of the district of Lafourche, are equally certain, equally well and specially described, so as to have been equally severed from the royal domain by the grant to M. Conway.

The objections are not aimed in verity at any uncertainty in the description and locality of the back lands intended by the Spanish grant, but at the liberality of the prince, at the extent of the grant, at the quantity included in the certain undeviating lines running by the given courses respectively, from the upper and lower corner on the Mississippi to the Amite, Iberville, and Lake Maurepas, the exterior boundary of the district of Lafourche.

The extent of this grant from the Mississippi to the Amite, Iberville, and Lake Maurepas, may make a difficulty in the minds of some men whose thoughts are restrained within a narrow compass, who are used to small tracts and sales of land for money by the acre, who are ignorant of the policy of Spain in bestowing the lands in the provinces in large quantities to men of distinction, to favorites, to persons who had performed military or civil services, or for the purpose of erecting useful establishments, or for introducing settlers, or for encouraging individual energy and enterprise, in seating and planting the lands, thereby to stimulate population, cultivation, production, the arts, and commerce, which constitute the wealth, and strength, and value of a province. The extent of this grant cannot be a matter of surprise or difficulty with those who reflect that Spain did not sell the Crown lands in the provinces for money, nor bargain by the arpent, nor look to wild lands belonging to the royal domain as a source of direct revenue. Grants by Spain in the provinces for eight leagues square, for ten leagues square, were frequent; and grants for thirty, fifty, or one hundred leagues square, are notorious. Witness the grants to the Baron de Bastrop, to the Marquis de Maison Rouge, to Miranda, to Austin, to the Duke of Alagon, to Count Punon Rostro, to Don Pedro de Vargas, and to various others.

The King of Spain and his council regarded people and private wealth in his provinces as better sources of revenue to fill the royal coffers than public lands in the rude state of nature.

II.—Construction of the acts of Congress.

The Attorney General Clifford will not allow that the act of Congress, approved April 18, 1814, (4 vol. Laws United States, by Bioren, chap. 681, p. 710,) confirmed the decisions of the commissioners made in favor of Wm. Conway, certificate No. 125, Daniel Clark, certificate No. 127, and Donelson and Scott, certificate No. 133, contained in the certified transcripts of decisions in favor of claimants then before the Congress, and on which that act was founded. And indeed says, (p. 44,) "No part of the act proposes to confirm any claim."

For the proper understanding of the act of 18th April, 1814, it is necessary and proper to look to the several acts of Congress for ascertaining and adjusting the private claims to lands in Louisiana, and the policy adopted to distinguish the lands belonging to individuals from the lands belonging to the United States, so that the public lands might be exposed to sale.

The acts upon this subject, which, being in pari materia, explain the duty and the intention of the Congress in enacting the two acts, the one approved on the 12th, and the other on the 18th of April, 1814, are the following:

Act of 1805, March 2d: "An act for ascertaining and adjusting the titles and claims to land within the Territory of Orleans, and district of Louisiana:" Vol. 3, Bioren, chap. 440, p. 652.

Act of 28th February, 1806: Vol. 4, Bioren, chap. 11, p. 6.

Act of 21st April, 1806: Vol. 4, Bioren, chap. 39, p. 50.

Act of 3d March, 1807: Vol. 4, Bioren, chap. 91, p. 111.

Act of 3d Match, 1811, entitled "an act providing for the final adjustment of claims to lands, and for the sale of the public lands in the territories of Orleans and Louisiana:" Vol. 4, chap. 323, p. 356.

Act of 12th April, 1814: Vol. 4, chap. 640, p. 680.

Act of 18th April, 1814: Vol. 4, chap. 681, p. 710.

The act of 1805 provides for ascertaining and adjusting the claims to lands in Louisiana by commissioners specially appointed to hear, determine, and confirm claims found to be good and valid; subject, however, to the final determination of the Congress upon the confirmations awarded in favor of claimants by the commissioners; to which end the commissioners were required to certify their decisions in favor of claimants, under their hands, (or of a majority of the board,) to the Secretary of the Treasury, to be by him laid before Congress for their determination thereon.

This act relates to claims by French and Spanish concessions, orders of survey, and grants, complete and incomplete.

Section 4 relates to legal French and Spanish grants, made and completed before the first day of October, 1800; and also to persons claiming by incomplete titles, described in the two first sections of this act of 1805.

To the persons having complete grants this 4th section gives the option, and to every claimant under incomplete grants, mentioned in the 1st and 2d section, the duty was imperative, to deliver to the register or recorder of the land office, on or before 1st March, 1806, "a notice in writing stating the nature and extent of his claims, together with a plat of the tract or tracts claimed."

And by this section all the claimants, as well by complete as by incomplete titles, were required also, on or before 1st March, 1806, to deliver to the register or recorder, "for the purpose of being recorded, every grant, order of survey, deed, conveyance, or other written evidence of his claim."

" Provided, however, that where lands are claimed by virtue of a complete French or Spanish grant as aforesaid, it shall not be necessary for the claimant to have any other evidence of his claim recorded, except the original grant or patent, together with the warrant or order of survey, and the plat; but all other conveyances, or deeds, shall be deposited with the register or recorder, to be by them laid before the commissioners."

As to this requirement about the plat subsequent acts dispensed with it, and provided for a survey and plat to be thereafter made, at the discretion of the commissioners, according to the circumstances.

For failing to comply with the requisitions of this fourth section of the act of 1805, the penalty was, as to the incomplete titles mentioned in the 1st and 2d sections, that they should become "barred and void;" as to complete grants, the title papers should never after be received as evidence "in any court of the United States against any grant derived from the United States."

Section 5 declared that two persons should be appointed by the President, to be approved by the Senate, for each district; who, together with the register of the district, should be commissioners for the respective districts, "for the purpose of ascertaining, within their respective districts, the rights of persons claiming under any French or Spanish grants, complete or incomplete, within the purview of the act."

"Each board, or a majority, shall, in their respective districts, have power to hear, and to decide, in a summary way, according to justice and equity, on all claims filed with the register or recorder, in conformity with the provisions of this act; and on all complete French and Spanish grants, the evidence of which, though not thus filed, may be found of record on the public records of such grants; which decisions shall be laid before Congress in the manner hereinafter directed, and be subject to their determination thereon."

The commissioners of each board respectively shall have power to appoint a clerk, "whose duty it shall be to enter in a book —— full and correct *minutes* of their proceedings, together with the evidence on which such decisions are made; which books and papers, on the dissolution of the boards, shall be deposited in the respective offices of the registers of the land offices, or of the recorder of the land titles of the district."

"And the said clerk shall prepare two transcripts of all the *decisions* made by the commissioners in favor of the claimants to land; both of which shall be *signed* by a majority of *said commissioners;* one of which shall be transmitted to the surveyor general, and the other to the Secretary of the Treasury."

The commissioners were also required "to make to the Secretary of the Treasury a full *report* of all the claims which may have been *rejected*, together with the substance of the evidence adduced in support thereof, and such remarks thereon as they may think proper; which *reports, together with the transcripts of the decisions of the commissioners in favor of the claimants,* shall be laid, by the Secretary of the Treasury, before Congress at their next ensuing meeting." (That is, next ensuing the receipt thereof by the Secretary of the Treasury, and for their determination thereon, as declared in the previous section.)

This section further declared, that the commissioners should not be bound to consider any such grant, warrant, or order of survey, as conclusive evidence of the title; but should inquire whether "the same is antedated, or otherwise fraudulent."

It is to be remembered, that there were, in Louisiana, three separate and distinct boards, with separate and distinct commissioners to each board. That the statute makes three classifications of the proceedings of each of these three boards of commissioners, viz:

1st. The minutes of all their decisions, as well in favor of the claimants as in rejecting claims; these minutes to be entered in a book by their respective clerks.

2d. *Certificates* of their decisions in *favor* of *claimants* to be prepared by the clerk, but authenticated by the commissioners themselves, certifying these transcripts of decisions in favor of claimants under their own proper signs manual, or by the signatures of a majority of them.

3d. *Reports* of the decisions rejecting claims to be made by the commissioners, with the substance of the evidence in support of the claims, together with the remarks of the commissioners thereon.

The first or original minutes to be deposited in the offices of the respective registers or recorders of the districts; the second, the *certificates* of their decisions in *favor* of claimants, were to be duplicated, each signed by the commissioners, or by a majority; one certified transcript from each district to be transmitted to the surveyor general of the district; the other to be transmitted to the Secretary of the Treasury; the third—*reports* of rejected claims, with the evidence and remarks—to be made to the Secretary of the Treasury.

The reports of rejected claims, evidence, and remarks thereon, together with the certified transcripts of decisions in favor of claimants, to be, by the Secretary of the Treasury, laid before the Congress, "subject to their determination thereon."

Thus, by the body and policy of this act, the registers or recorders of the land offices in each of the districts, the surveyor general of each district, and the Secretary of the Treasury, (the head of all the land offices,) were severally and respectively officially informed, and furnished with authentic evidence, of all the decisions of the commissioners in favor of the claimants to land within their respective districts.

The 7th section of this act made it the duty of the surveyor general to cause the lands belonging to the United States within the territory of Orleans, to which the Indian title then was or should thereafter be extinguished, "to be surveyed and divided, as nearly as the nature of the country will admit, in the same manner and under the same regulations as is provided by law in relation to the lands of the United States northwest of the river Ohio, and above the mouth of the Kentucky river."

The next act upon the subject was approved 28th February, 1806, (4 vol. Laws U. S., by Bioren, chap. xi, p. 6,) entitled "An act extending the powers of the surveyor general to the territory of Louisiana, and for other purposes."

This act extended the powers of the surveyor general over the whole territory of Louisiana—the act of 1805, sect. 7th, having extended the powers of the surveyor general of lands south of the State of Tennessee over the district of Orleans only.

He was required to cause to be executed "such surveys as may be hereafter authorized by law, or as he may be directed to execute by the commissioners appointed for the purpose of ascertaining the titles and claims to land within the territory aforesaid," &c.

The second section enacted "that all plats of surveys, and all papers and documents pertaining, or which did pertain, to the office of surveyor general under the Spanish government, or to any other office heretofore established or authorized for the purpose of executing or recording surveys of lands within the said limits, shall be delivered to the principal deputy," (whose office and residence is by law required to be in Louisiana.)

Section 3 repeals so much of the act of 1805 as made it the duty of claimants "to deliver a plot of the tracts claimed by him" to the recorder, so far as relates to claimants whose tracts had not been surveyed by the proper officer under the Spanish government prior to the 28th December, 1803; and the commissioners were authorized to direct a survey of any claim to be made by the officer exercising the power of surveyor general, "as they may think necessary for the purpose of deciding on claims presented for their decision."

"All tracts of land, the titles to which may be ultimately *confirmed* by Congress, in conformity with the provisions of the act above mentioned, (1805,) shall, prior to the issuing of patents, be *resurveyed*, if judged to be necessary, under the authority of the person exercising the powers of surveyor general, and at the expense of the parties."

Under the effect of this statute, it is clear that, if the commissioners desired any other survey and plat than that filed by the parties, they could have caused a survey to be made.

The plat could do no more than give notice of the nature and extent of the claim, and if not satisfactory to the commissioners, they had the authority expressly given to cause a survey. It seems, however, that the Attorney General gave himself great labor, in his opinion as printed, about an immaterial matter; for he shows that these several parties claiming under the grant to Conway did file a plat shewing the nature and extent of their claims, together with the original grant, order of survey, and survey, and deeds and conveyances made before the cession of the country to the United States, all showing the fronts on the Mississippi, and the courses running back in depth to the Iberville, or Amite, or Maurepas, being different names for the same stream. (See Attorney General's Opinion, pp. 4, 5, 6, 7, 8, 9, 10, 11, 12, and 13.)

It seems, in reason, law, and equity, very immaterial under what authority Lafon acted, whether under the public authority of Governor Claiborne, or under the private authority of the owners of the land.

The Attorney General seems to be of opinion that the executive instructions of the President to Governor Claiborne could countervail the act of Congress; that the authority of the President to direct the *manner* of exercising the powers vested in the governor by the Congress authorized the President to repeal the powers themselves; and that the President could prohibit the holders under a complete Spanish grant from causing surveys of their own lands. To maintain such propositions is above the might of the Attorney General, as far as an honest and a wise man is above the might of a prince.

The laws and officers of the laws of a country transferred from one sovereignty and jurisdiction to another, (whether by conquest or by cession, can make no difference in this respect,) continue until alteied, modified, or abrogated by the new sovereign.—Campbell *vs*. Hall, I Cowper, 209; 5th resolve, Calvin's case, 7 Coke, 17, (b.)

By the act of 21st April, 1806, (vol. 4, page 50, Bioren's ed.,) modifications were made in relation to claims more favorable to certain descriptions of claimants than the act of 1805.

By the 5th section of this act of 21st April, 1806, the time for delivering "notices in writing, and written evidences of claims to land," was prolonged; and the penalties "provided by the 4th section of the act to which this is a supplement," were re-enacted.

The 7th section relates to the powers of "the commissioners appointed for the purpose of ascertaining the rights of persons claiming lands in the territories of Orleans and Louisiana," and gives facilities for taking oral evidence either in support of, or in opposition to claims.

Section 8 enacts "that each of the boards aforesaid shall prepare, and cause to be prepared, the reports and transcripts which by law they are directed to make to the Secretary of the Treasury, in conformity with such forms as he may prescribe; and they shall also, in their several proceedings and *decisions*, conform to such instructions as the Secretary of the Treasury may, with the approbation of the President of the United States, transmit to them in relation thereto."

Section 9 requires the surveyor of the public lands, south of Tennessee, to appoint a principal deputy for each of these two land districts of the territory of Orleans, whose duty it shall be to reside and keep an office in said districts respectively, to execute, or cause to be executed by other deputies, such surveys as have been or may be authorized by law; "or, as the commissioners aforesaid may direct, to file and record all such surveys, to form as far as practicable connected draughts of the lands granted in the district, so as to exhibit the lands remaining vacant."

This section farther shows, that to exhibit the lands belonging to the private rights of property secured by the treaty of cession, and the lands remaining vacant and so belonging to the public domain of the United States, was the end and aim of the Government in appointing these boards of commissioners.

Section 11 authorized the President to offer for sale so much of the public lands "as shall have been surveyed in conformity with the provisions of the act (of 1805) to which this is a supplement."

The act of 1807, March 3, entitled (Laws U. S., Bioren's ed., vol. 4, chap. 91, p. 111) "An act respecting claims to land in the territories of Orleans and Louisiana," declares in section 4, that in certain descriptions of cases the decisions of the commissioners shall be final upon claims under the French and Spanish laws, usages, and customs, when in favor of the claimant, for a tract not exceeding a league square, and not including a lead mine or salt spring.

Section 5 extended the time for giving notices and filing evidences of all claims.

Section 6 required the commissioners to transmit to the Secretary of the Treasury and the surveyor general "transcripts of the *final* decisions made in favor of claimants by virtue of this act; and they shall deliver to the party a certificate stating the circumstances of the case, and *that he is entitled to a patent* for a tract of land therein designated; which certificate shall be filed with the proper register or recorder within twelve months after date, who shall thereupon (a plat of the tract of land therein designated being previously filed with him, or transmitted to him by the officer acting as surveyor general, in the manner hereinafter provided) issue a certificate in favor of the party, which certificate being transmitted to the Secretary of the Treasury, shall entitle the party to a patent, to be issued in like manner as is provided by law for issuing patents for public lands lying in other territories of the United States."

Section 7 enacts that the tracts of land thus granted by "the commissioners shall be surveyed at the expense of the parties, under the direction of the surveyor general, in all cases where an authenticated plat of the land, as surveyed under the authority of the officer acting as surveyor general under the French, Spanish, or American Governments respectively, shall not have been filed with the proper register or recorder, or shall not appear of record on the public records of said territories of Orleans and Louisiana. The said commissioners shall also be authorized, whenever they may think it necessary, to direct the surveyor general, or officer acting as such, to cause any tract of land already duly surveyed to be resurveyed at the expense of the United States. And the surveyor general shall transmit general and particular plats of the tracts of land to the proper register or recorder, and also copies of said plats to the Secretary of the Treasury."

Section 8 enacts that the commissioners shall arrange all the claims *not finally* confirmed by the fourth section of this act into three classes: "first, claims which, in the opinion of the commissioners, ought to be *confirmed,* in conformity with the *several acts of Congress* for ascertaining and adjusting the titles and claims to lands within the territories of Orleans and Louisiana; secondly, claims which, though not embraced by the provisions of said acts, ought, nevertheless, in the opinion of the commissioners, to be *confirmed* in conformity with the laws, usages, and customs of the Spanish government; third, claims which neither are embraced by the provisions of said act, nor ought, in the opinion of the commissioners, to be confirmed in conformity with the laws, usages, and customs of the Spanish government.

"And the said report and reports being in *other respects made in conformity* with the forms *prescribed* according to law by the *Secretary of the Treasury,* shall by him be laid before Congress for their final determination thereon, in the manner and at the time heretofore prescribed by law."

Taking all these several acts together, it will be seen—

That by the 4th section of the act of 1807, certain claims therein described, and not exceeding one league square, when decided in favor of the claimants, were final and conclusive against the United States, and patents were to issue to the claimants in the manner directed by the sixth and seventh sections of the act, without any confirmation by the Congress, and without more ado than what was directed in those sections.

As to the claims not so finally decided by the commissioners, and so conclusively confirmed under the 4th section, they consisted of claims exceeding and not exceeding one league square; claims by complete grants, and by incomplete grants. These the commissioners were to arrange into three classes, according to the act of 1807, to be certified according to the acts of 1805 and 1806, and of 1807, subject to the determination of Congress thereon.

The classes of claims decided by the commissioners in favor of the claimants were, by the 5th section of the act of 1805, the 8th section of the act of 21st April, 1806, and the 8th section of the act of 1807, to be transmitted by the commissioners of the respective boards, certified under their signatures, in which certificates so to be made by the commissioners, they were bound to include all decisions in favor of claimants; and by the 6th section of the act of 1807, the duty of the commissioners to certify in their transcripts the final decisions in favor of claimants under the act of 1807, section 4, was but repeated.

The act of 1805 required all decisions in favor of claimants to be *certified* to the Secretary of the Treasury to be laid before Congress. Rejected claims were to be *reported* by the commissioners, with the evidence, and their remarks.

By the combined effect of the 5th section of the act of 1805, the 8th section of the act of 21st April, 1806, the 8th section of the act of 1807, and the 4th and 6th sections of the act of 1807, the certified transcripts of decisions by the commissioners, in favor of claimants, included—

1. The decisions upon claims not exceeding one league square, made final and conclusive by the fourth section of the act of 1807, not requiring any farther determination by the Congress, upon which patents were ordered by the sixth section of that act, but nevertheless to be included in the certified transcripts of decisions in favor of claimants, ordered by the fifth section of the act of 1805, and by the 8th section of the act of 1806, and the 8th section of the act of 1807.

2. All other decisions in favor of claimants, arranged into classes, according to the 8th section of the act of 1807; the one, claims on grants, warrants, and concessions, complete and incomplete, which ought to be confirmed, because good and valid under the Spanish laws, usages, and customs, and likewise included in, and conformable to, the provisions of the several acts of Congress; the other, claims by grants, concessions, order of survey, &c., which ought to be confirmed, though *not embraced* in the provisions of the acts of Congress, these claims being, nevertheless, "in conformity with the laws, usages, and customs of the Spanish government;" these two last classes subject to the review and determination of the Congress.

In addition to the certified transcripts of decisions in favor of the claimants, the commissioners were required, by the 5th section of the act of 1805, and 8th section of the act of 1807, to report the rejected claims, with the evidence, and the remarks of the commissioners thereon.

In anticipation of the certified transcripts of the decisions of the commissioners in favor of claimants, the Congress had passed the act approved March 3d, 1811, entitled "An act providing for the final adjustment of claims to land, and for the sale of the public lands in the territories of Orleans and Louisiana," &c., (4 vol., by Bioren, chap. 323, page 356,) in which, after alluding to the decisions of the commissioners, enacts and provides that, "till after the decision of Congress thereon, no tract of land shall be offered for sale the claim to which has been filed in due time, and according to law presented, for the purpose of being investigated by the commissioners." By the fifth section every claimant, by a French or Spanish grant, "confirmed by the commissioners," for a tract of land "bordering on any river, creek, bayou, or water-course, and not exceeding forty arpens in depth, French measure, shall be entitled to preference in becoming purchaser of any vacant land adjacent to and back of his own tract, not exceeding forty arpens."

Before the passage of this act these claims now under consideration had been investigated and confirmed by the commissioners, viz., in the year 1806. The duty of Congress, therefore, to make their final determination, in a reasonable time after the claims decided in favor of claimants should be certified and laid before the Congress, was plain and impressive.

The commissioners performed their duties, certified their decisions in favor of claimants, which were laid before the Congress, by the Secretary of the Treasury, in January, 1812; and also reported the rejected claims, with the evidence and remarks.

It is to be observed that the treaty of cession is superior in obligation to any act of Congress, if in conflict with the treaty.

The Congress have the power to acknowledge and confirm, as against the United States, the validity of private rights, but not the rightful power to annul or impair the vested private rights and interests in the lands within the pale and protection of the treaty:

The Congress of the United States, and the Government of the United States, were, and are, by the ratification of the treaty and the acceptance of the possession of the ceded territory, bound by the sacred faith of treaties, which secures the safety and repose of nations, to acknowledge, respect, protect, and confirm, as against the Government, all those private rights and interests in lands in the ceded territory, which fall under the stipulation of the third article of the treaty, and within the meaning, sense, and spirit of the cession, as explained and expressed in the first and second articles. The sovereignty and public domain, public property, "public lots and squares, vacant lands, and all public buildings, fortifications, barracks, and other edifices, *which are not private property*," were the subjects ceded. Had the treaty of cession been silent on the subject of private rights, the law of nations, and the principles of justice, of universal obligation, would have protected private rights and interests lawfully acquired, (whether complete or incomplete,) under the laws, usages, and customs of the sovereign having the domain and jurisdiction at the time.

With these preliminaries we come to the questions—What use has Congress made of their power, reserved in the acts of 1805 and 1807, to review the decisions of the commissioners? Have the Congress reversed the decisions of the commissioners? Have the Congress slept for upwards of thirty three years since the transcripts of the decisions in favor of claimants, certified by the commissioners, were laid before them, by the Secretary of the Treasury, for their determination? Or have the Congress confirmed the decisions of the commissioners, which were made in favor of the claimants?

These questions are answered by the acts of 12th and 18th April, 1814; which, taken together, amount to a confirmation of all the decisions of the commissioners in favor of claimants then transmitted to the Congress in the certified transcripts of the decisions of the commissioners, as well on incomplete as on complete titles, whether not exceeding or exceeding one league square.

The act of 12th April, 1814, entitled "An act for the final adjustment of land titles in the State of Louisiana and Territory of Missouri," (vol. 4, chap. 640, page 680, of Bioren's ed.,) confirmed all decisions of the commissioners in favor of claimants, upon incomplete grants, not exceeding one league square; and went farther to confirm (by section 2) claims not confirmed by the commissioners, "merely because the tracts of land claimed were not inhabited on the 20th December, 1803." That condition of habitation, so annexed by the Congress in the instructions to the commissioners, was in conflict with terms of the cession, as explained in art. 1 and 2; therefore the Congress confirmed those claims so situated.

These confirmations included tracts of land which had been then surveyed, as well as tracts of land which had not then been surveyed—tracts whereof plats had been filed with the commissioners, or register, or recorder, as well as tracts whereof plats had not been so filed; the third and fourth sections of this act made provision for surveys to be executed and returned, and patents to issue in cases where no surveys had been previously made.

Next in the order of confirmations of claims came the act of 18th April, 1814, entitled "An act concerning certificates of confirmation of claims to lands in the State of Louisiana."—(4 vol., chap. 681, page 710.)

This act embraces two classes of claims, which had been decided by the commissioners in favor of claimants:

1st. "All cases where certificates of confirmation to lands, in either of the land districts of Louisiana, "have been issued agreeably with the provisions of the act passed March 3d, 1807, and which were directed to be filed with the proper register of the land office within twelve months after date."

This description is full, exact, and complete, wanting nothing farther to identify them; definite, without doubt, or room for mistake; whioh were final and conclusive, not subject to determination of Congress.

2d. "And on claims which are included in the transcripts of decisions made in favor of claimants, and transmitted to the Secretary of the Treasury."

This contains another description of claims, included in the transcripts then before the Congress, confirmed by the commissioners, certified under their hands, and transmitted to the Secretary of the Treasury, subject to the determination of Congress, and laid before Congress for their determination.

The act of April 18th, 1814, declares, "that in all cases where certificates of confirmation to lands lying in either of the land districts established by law in the *State* of Louisiana, have been issued agieeably with the provisions of the act entitled ' An act respecting claims to land in the territories of Orleans and Louisiana,' passed the third of March, 1807, and which were directed to be filed with the proper register of the land office within twelve months after date, and on claims which are included in the transcript of decisions made in favor of claimants and transmitted to the Secretary of the Treasury," &c. This includes a genus and two species.

The genus is, all cases of certificates of confirmation to lands in either of the land districts in the State of Louisiana, which have been issued agreeably with the act of 3d March, 1807.

This definition of certificates of confirmation to lands in Louisiana, and issued agreeably with the act of 3d of March, 1807, was necessary to distinguish this genus from the genera of land claims and certificates of confirmations in all other land districts of the United States.

The first species is formed by superadding the specific difference to the genus, so as to divide the species from the genus; the genus and the specific difference being the proper constituent parts of the species.

The first species is described by the words "and which were directed to be filed with the proper register of the land office within twelve months after date." The word " and" connects the specific difference with the genus, and defines clearly and identically that species of certificates of confirmation, which the commissioners had authoritatively pronounced and issued agreeably with the fourth and sixth sections of that act of 1807, being final and conclusive in effect, requiring no determination by Congress thereon.

The second species is formed by superadding another specific difference to the genus; which other species differs from the former. This second species is defined by the words " and on claims which are included in the transcript of decisions made in favor of claimants and transmitted to the Secretary of the Treasury." The word " and" connects this second species with the genus.

These two species differed from each other. The one species, certified under the sixth section of the act of 1807, were final and conclusive; not subject to be reviewed or reversed by Congress; directed to be filed with the proper registers within twelve months from their date, entitling the claimants to have American patents forthwith; and were not exceeding one league square. The other species, certified under the eighth section of the act of 1807—not final and conclusive, but expressly subject to the review and determination of Congress; laid before Congress for their determination; upon which American patents could not issue, until Congress approved; and were *exceeding* as well as *not exceeding* one league square in various instances.

The word "issued" employed in the general description of "all cases of certificates of confirmation to lands lying in either of the land districts established by law in the State of Louisiana," cannot limit and confine the description to one species of decisions in favor of claimants in preference to another, but includes those which were not final and conclusive against the United States, as well as those which were final. "Issued" means descended; produced by any cause; passed out of any place; run out in lines; sent out judicially or authoritatively; sent forth; sprung from.

The decisions of the commissioners in favor of claimants were certificates of confirmation, descended from the powers given by law to the commissioners; produced by those powers; sent out by the commissioners authoritatively, in compliance with their powers and duties; run out in lines signed and certified by the commissioners of the respective districts; sent forth from the office of the commissioners; sprung from them; issued to the Secretary of the Treasury; issued to the surveyor general of the district; issued to any claimant, at his request, in whose favor the commissioners had decided, whether the decision was final and conclusive, or subject to the future determination of Congress; and also sent forth or issued from the commissioners to the registers of the land offices.

The differences between the certificates of confirmation, coming within the purview of the fourth and sixth sections of the act of 1807, and those coming within the purview of the first, second, fifth, and eighth sections of that act, are: certificates of confirmation within the purview of the fourth and sixth sections, were final and conclusive against the United States, and stated on their face " that the claimants were entitled to a patent for a tract of land therein designated." The final effect of such decisions, and that the claimant was entitled to a patent, were matters decided by the commissioners, entered in the minutes, there signed, and so certified; whereas the other certificates of confirmation were not final and conclusive, but subject to the determination of Congress, stated the claimant, the tract of land claimed, the evidence in support of it, that the land so claimed was the property of the claimant, and that the board "do hereby confirm his said claim;" omitting the statement as to the final effect, and that the claimant was entitled to a patent.

The Attorney General Clifford labors very hard to read the act of 18th April, 1814, as if certain, important, effective, significant, words of the statute had not been inserted; to that end, he supposes an elision, transposes words and members of the sentence, reads it with an ellipsis, interlards words between the dislocations; and by transpositions, elisions, luxations, transformations, inlarding, interlacing, and rhetorical ellipsis, he comes to the conclusion that the statute has no other nor more extensive signification than if it had said, for the certificates of confirmation issued to claimants under the *sixth section* of the act of March the third, 1807, omitting the other sections of that same act.

This mode, adopted by the Attorney General to accomplish his desire, is after the manner of Peter, Martin, and Jack, in construing their father's will, as reported in A Tale of a Tub, whereby they evaded the meaning, commands, and injunctions of the will. When they could not find what they desired totidem verbis in the will, they tried the expedient of totidem syllabis; then by totidem literis; and lastly added a codicil. By means of these learned devices, of culling words, syllables, or letters, and stringing them together in such order as best suited their purpose, with the help of the codicil, they allowed themselves shoulder knots, flame-colored satin linings, silver fringe, gold lace, and embroidery, with Indian figures, contrary to the meaning of their father's will. Thus they claimed and exercised, as heirs-general of their father, the power to make and add certain clauses in the will, or cut them out for public emolument, and came to conclusions contrary to the will totidem verbis, or else great loss to the public would follow.

The Attorney General Cliffoid, to sustain his construction, seems to forget that the act of 18th April, 1814, does not require that all the lands, for which patents were to be given under that act, shall necessarily be thereafter surveyed by the principal deputy surveyor of the district upon certificates sent out to him by the register of the district, but only in cases "where the lands have not been already surveyed according to law." Lands which had been lawfully surveyed by the French, or Spanish, or American authorities, or where plats had been filed with the commissioners, or where the surveyor general or the commissioners themselves had caused a survey or a *resurvey*, (as authorized to do by the seventh section of the act of March 3d, 1807; by the third section of the act of 28th February, 1806; and also by the ninth section of the act of 21st April, 1806,) were not necessarily to be resurveyed upon certificates sent out by the registers.

It has been shown that those acts had expressly provided for surveys of all lands to be made by the surveyor general, or person acting as such, not only upon the final certificates of confirmation under the fourth and sixth sections of the act of 1807, but in all cases where an authenticated plat of the land, as surveyed under the authority of the French, Spanish, or American Governments, shall not have been filed with the proper register or recorder, or shall not appear of record on the public records of the said territories of Orleans and Louisiana;" moreover had expressly authorized the commissioners, whenever they may think it necessary, to direct the surveyor general, or officer acting as such, to cause any tract of land already surveyed to be resurveyed (as in seventh section of act of 1807;) or to cause surveys to be made, (as in third section of act of 28th February, and ninth section of act of 21st April,

1805.) By these acts the surveyor general "was directed to transmit general and particular plats of the tracts of land thus surveyed to the proper register or recorder;" and to "transmit copies of the said plats to the Secretary of the Treasury."

The expressions of the act of 18th April, 1814, as to the surveys and return thereof, "with the original certificates," do not apply to any cases where the tracts of land had already been surveyed, and even in cases where surveys had not been made; wherefore the registers were required to send out the certificates, "together with the proper descriptions of the tracts to be surveyed, wherein the quantity, locality, and connexion, when practicable, with each other, shall be stated," such surveys cannot be confined solely and exclusively to such certificates as were granted as final and conclusive under the fourth and sixth sections of the act of 1807. The confirmations spoken of are not confined to those two sections of the act. The whole act of 1807 is alluded to in the act of 18th April, 1814; all the sections are included, and not two only in exclusion of all others.

The Attorney General's construction supposes all the words in the ten lines of the printed statute, beginning with the word "that" and ending with the words "Secretary of the Treasury," to be descriptive of one and the same species of claims. Such construction cuts short the beneficial operation and equity of the act, and renders the words "and on claims which are included in the transcripts of decisions made in favor of claimants, and transmitted to the Secretary of the Treasury," useless and inoperative. Moreover, to effect the purpose of such continuous description of the same species, and the same idea, by such exuberant loquacity, the words "and on claims," which are interposed between the words "after date" and the words "which are included," should be stricken out, as interruptions to the propriety of speech, as well as to the unity of thought.

The first and second sections of the act of 18th April, 1814, in providing for surveys, and returns thereof, in cases "where the lands have not been already surveyed," do not limit and confine the operation of that act solely to such unsurveyed lands. They are remedial words, to extend the benefits of the act; not to limit, curtail, and do away with the previous provisions intended to preserve the faith of the treaty, and the policy of ascertaining the private rights and the public domain.

To limit and confine the operation of that act solely to confirmations which were final and conclusive, under the fourth and sixth sections of the act of 1807, would be as absurd as to confine its operation solely to the cases of unsurveyed lands, to cases of incomplete grants.

The act of 18th April, 1814, must be construed by applying its several and respective parts and provisions to cases respectively to which the several and distinct provisions are appropriate and pertinent. The statute is not to be used, like the bed of Procrustes, to chop or stretch all cases to the one and the same standard, however differing in features, lineaments, proportions, and circumstances, confirmed by the decisions of the commissioners in favor of the claimants. The provisions of the statute, as to the several classes and differences in the claims, must be applied, reddenda singula singulis, equitably, discreetly, according to reason and due discrimination, so that all the parts of the act shall have effect and operation, to the end that the faith of the treaty may be preserved pure and undefiled.

The several statutes of 1805, two of 1806, and of 1807, are all made upon the same subject, for the same reason and purpose, and in continuation; the latter in continuance of the former; and therefore all are to be considered in the construction of one another, and as if the latter had repeated and re-enacted the former, so far as congruous.

Baily *vs.* Martin, 1 Ventris, 246.

XIX Viner. Statutes, (E. 6,) pl. 109, and cases cited in the margin, page 523.

"A man ought not to rest upon the letter only (of a statute,) nam qui hæret in litera bæret in cortice; but he ought to rely upon the sense which is temperated and guided by equity; and therein he reaps the fruit of the law; for as a nut consists of a shell and a kernel, so every statute consists of the letter and the sense; and as the kernel is the fruit of the nut, so the sense is the fruit of the statute."

Stowell *vs.* Zouche, Plowden, 363.

Esyston *vs.* Studd, Plowden, 465, 467.

The decisions of the commissioners in favor of claimants were first written in the books of the respective boards of commissioners of the several and respective districts, certified there by the sign manual of the commissioners, or of a majority, and deposited, upon the dissolution of the board, in the office of the register of the land office of the district. All others, although certified and authenticated by the signatures of the commissioners, whether in the office of the Secretary of the Treasury, or in the hall of the one or the other house of Congress, or in the office of the Surveyor General, or in the hands of the claimants, were transcripts, certified by the commissioners themselves, as the law directed.

In legal language, all were originals, all alike, all certified alike, all counterparts, just as the parts of an indenture, quadri partite, having the same words, same signatures, same authentications and solemnities, all are originals; one part is as much an original as any other. Yet one must have been first written and the others transcribed, otherwise they would not have been exactly alike, and counterparts; neither could all be executed and delivered at one and the same instant, but in succession; yet, when finished, all are originals.

The sixth section of the act of 1807 directed the commissioners imperatively "to deliver to the party a certificate, stating the circumstances of the case, and that he is entitled to a patent;" and these were to be delivered to the proper register within twelve months after date. But this did not prohibit the commissioners from giving to claimants, in whose favor they made decisions—not final, but subject to the ultimate determination of Congress—certificates of their decisions, although not entitling them to patents until the determination of Congress; and, in practice, the commissioners conformed to that which was so reasonably

6

expected by claimants placed under the circumstances of having their titles called in question by the new jurisdiction to which they had been transferred, and to whom they had been compelled to deliver their title papers. The eighth section of this same act required these confirmations also to be certified to the surveyor general, to the Secretary of the Treasury.

The transcripts, for the Secretary of the Treasury, for the surveyor general, and books deposited with the proper registers, and the decisions delivered to the claimants respectively, all agreed, were all alike certified by the commissioners or a majority; for the clerk had no authority to authenticate transcripts, no authority but to enter the minutes of the decisions in a book, and to prepare the transcripts to be signed and certified by the commissioners.

The act of 1807 does not baptize any of these certified copies or transcripts of the decisions in favor of claimants, "certificates of confirmation," (eo nomine.) But, in fact and law, they were so, in respect of the decisions, whether final and conclusive in favor of the claimants, or subject to the determination of Congress. The forms of the decisions, as entered, were confirmations; that form was uniform as to all decisions in favor of claimants, whether final and conclusive, or only sub modo, subject to the determination of Congress; the transcripts certified and laid before Congress were so. The first act of 1805, and all the supplements, alluded to the decisions in favor of claimants as intended confirmations. Even before the time appointed for the commissioners to meet and hold their sessions, the law called their decisions in favor of claimants, when made, confirmations by operation of the decisions, (but subject to the review and determination of Congress;) required them to be certified for the determination of Congress; and declared they should be authenticated by the certificates of the commissioners themselves, under their signatures, or of a majority.

After the respective boards of commissioners had completed their proceedings in examining and deciding on the claims, they did certify their decisions in favor of claimants as directed to do by the 5th section of the original act of 1805, March 2d, and the supplements of 21st April, 1806, sections 5 and 8, and of 3d March, 1807, sections 6 and 8, signed by their own hands and certificates to the transcripts, one of which was transmitted to the surveyor general, another to the Secretary of the Treasury, which he laid before Congress for their determination, according to the directions of the acts of Congress before mentioned.

The thirteenth Congress, disposed to do their duty in relation to the transcripts of the decisions of the commissioners made in favor of claimants, then before them, passed the act of 18th April, 1814. That act applies to the "certificates of confirmation" then before Congress, upon which they were acting, which were in their power and possession, which they saw, had inspected, and deliberated upon; not to certificates which they had not seen, which were not in their possession or power, but in the hands of individuals.

. The act of 18th April, 1814, applies "in all cases where certificates of confirmation for lands in the State of Louisiana, certified in the transcripts described in the act, whether certified in obedience to the 6th section, or in obedience to the 8th section, of the act of March 3d, 1807. The decisions certified under the 8th section, made in favor of claimants, were within the predicate of the act of 18th April, 1814, equally with those certified under the 6th section. The statute of 18th April, 1814, does not designate the 6th section, to the exclusion of the 8th. All cases of 'certificates of confirmation' for lands lying in the State of Louisiana, contained in the transcripts of the decisions then before the Congress, and in their power and possession, which had been transmitted to the Secretary of the Treasury and laid before them, are within the purview of the act. The maxim is, 'Qui omne dicit, nihil excludit; generale dictum, generaliter est intelligendum.' "

Co., 2 Inst., 81.

When the act of 18th April, 1814, passed, the commissioners of each of the land districts in the State of Louisiana had respectively issued " certificates of confirmation to lands lying in each of the land districts established by law in the State of Louisiana," to the surveyor general, to the Secretary of the Treasury, and to the registers of the land districts. All these certificates of confirmation had been issued by the commissioners from their office, all certified by them in like manner, all issued in obedience to the directions of the law and the instructions of the Secretary of the Treasury. By the means of the certificates of confirmation so issued by the commissioners, and so deposited with the register, the surveyor general, and the Secretary of the Treasury, (who was and is the head of the Land office,) these several and respective officers had authentic evidence in their respective offices whereby to perform their several and respective parts in relation to patents to be issued upon the certificates of confirmation to lands lying in the several land districts. One of the transcripts of all the confirmations, certified by the commissioners of each of the land districts established by law in the State of Louisiana, was laid before Congress for the special purpose of their determination thereon. The " certificates of confirmation " contained in the transcripts then before the Congress, and upon which they deliberated, and determined, are the certificates of confirmation alluded to in the act of 18th April, 1814, and not the several certificates delivered to the claimants themselves, which the Congress did not see, and of which they could have no knowledge, except by reading the certificates of confirmation laid before them, and upon which they acted and made their determination. The decisions made in favor of claimants, then before the Congress, to them certified by the commissioners, for the determination of the Congress thereon, are the certificates of confirmation alluded to in the act, described in the act, named, called, and acknowledged by the act, as " certificates of confirmation " which had been issued, produced, lawfully procreated, and brought into existence by the commissioners, and presented to the sight of the Congress, and then in their presence for their determination thereon. These are the " certificates of confirmation," the consequences and issues of the decisions made in favor of claimants by the commissioners, which are acknowledged as lawful by the act of 18th April, 1814, and as entitling the claimants under the Spanish or French grants, concessions, orders of survey, or warrants, (whether their titles were complete or incomplete at the time of the cession of Louisiana to the United States,) to be confirmed and quieted by American patents. All these certificates of confirmation, without exception, are acknowledged by the Congress in their act of 18th April, 1814, as entitled to American patents.

It seems to be an obliquity and perversity towards the claimants in whose favor the commissioners had made, entered, and certified their decisions, to refuse to apply the words, sense, and meaning of the act of 18th April, 1814, to all the certificates of confirmation within the genus of confirmations mentioned in that act, contained in the transcript certified by the commissioners, and then actually before the Congress as the subjects of their deliberation; and to insist upon confining the act solely to one species, thereby making the Congress to have neglected their duty, depart from things before them to things unseen by them; to have left undone things which they ought to have done, for the sake of things which did not need their concurrence; thereby to clip and mar the general words, justice, and equity of the act.

The Congress, on the 18th April, 1814, acted upon the certificates of confirmations, which the commissioners had certified in obedience to the law, and the instructions of the Secretary given to the commissions in pursuance of law; which certified decisions in favor of claiman s were intended, ordered, and designed from the beginning to be subject to the determination of Congress.

The form of the decisions by the commissioners, in cases decided in favor of claimants, stated the claimant; the tract of land claimed was accurately described; the derivation of title was mentioned; and that from the proof it appeared " that said land has become the property of the present claimant, *the board do hereby confirm* his said claim."

This is the exact form of the certificates of confirmation in each of the cases, of Donaldson & Scott, certificate, No. 133; of Daniel Clark, certificate No. 127; and William Conway, certificate No. 125; claiming under the grants to Maurice Conway of 1774 and 1777, called the Houmas grant.

As the certificates of the decisions of the commissioners in favor of claimants contained an express confirmation, it was not necessary for the Congress to enter a formal confirmation. It was necessary for the Congress, in case the decision of the commissioners in favor of a claimant was disapproved, to enter a reversal. In the second section of the act of 12th April, 1814, the Congress did reverse the decisions of the commissioners made *against* claimants in a class of cases, and declared a confirmation of all those claims.

In all the cases presented by claimants to the commissioners for hearing and determination, the claimant was one party and the United States were the other party, actually appearing and represented by agents specially appointed to investigate all claims, one to each board, and to oppose all claims which said investigating agents" may deem fraudulent and unfounded." (See said act of 1805, sect. 6.) The proceedings before the commissioners were ordered, conducted, and superintended by the United States. The commissioners proceeded, under instructions, not only as to the *forms* of their proceedings, but also as to their *decisions*, according to the eighth section of the act of 1806, before mentioned.

The decisions in favor of claimants, made by commissioners so proceeding, so instructed, so attended by special agents of Government appointed to investigate all claims, and to oppose such as they supposed unfounded, containing, in the body of their decisions, certificates of confirmation, are entitled to the highest respect, if not reversed and set aside by the Congress.

The commissioners heard and determined the claims under this Houmas grant to Maurice Conway, gave decisions in favor of the claimants upon their claims, extending in depth to Lake Maurepas, Iberville, and Amite; entered their awards of confirmations, and certified these confirmations to the Secretary of the Treasury, who laid them before the Congress for their determination. The thirteenth Congress took up the certified confirmations so laid before them, and passed the act of 18th April, 1814.

It is not pretended that the Congress reversed, set aside, annulled, or disapproved these decisions of the commissioners in favor of the claimants under the Houmas grant, expressly confirming their claims as good and valid. That the Congress, in April, 1814, did consider and deliberate upon the transcripts containing all the decisions of the commissioners in favor of claimants in the several districts of Louisiana, is clearly and undeniably apparent by the two acts of the Congress, the one passed 12th April, the other 18th April, 1814. That the Congress did not reverse, set aside, or disapprove those confirmations so certified by the commissioners is apparent by the inspection of those statutes. What, then, did the Congress determine upon them? What did the Congress do?

Attorney General Clifford says, (in page 44, of his printed opinion,) " No part of the act of 18th April, 1814, *proposes to confirm any claim,* but merely authorizes, under certain prescribed rules, the issuing of patents in a class of cases specially designated, and for lands which had been previously *confirmed* under the law of 1807." Again, he says, (page 47, of his printed opinion,) " The claims that had been brought before the board on complete and perfect titles, were not confirmed, for the reason, unquestionably, that they required no confirmation from the Government of the United States. Such lands had been severed from the domain of the crown of Spain before the treaty of cession, and had become private property, and were alike protected by the law of nations and by the terms of the treaty. These titles, therefore, must stand or fall upon their own merits."

. From these quotations it appears, that Attorney General Clifford has affirmed these propositions as veritable: 1st, that the act authorizing

American patents to issue upon Spanish concessions and grants, does not propose to confirm any claim; 2d, that claims by complete grants were not confirmed, by that act, unquestionably because they wanted none; 3d, that incomplete Spanish grants were not severed from the domain of the Crown of Spain, were not protected by the law of nations, and the treaty; therefore they stood in need of confirmation by the United States.

The first proposition, that to authorize American patents to issue upon Spanish claims, is not a confirmation of the Spanish claims, as affirmed by Attorney General Clifford, is a proof that the affirmant did not understand the legal meaning of a confirmation.

" Confirmation is the approbation, or assent to, an estate already created, which, as far as in the confirmer's power, makes it good and valid ; so that the confirmation doth not regularly create an estate ; such words may be mingled in the confirmation as may create and enlarge an estate, but that is by force of such words as are foreign to the business of confirmation, and by their own force and power tend to create the estate." Gilbert's tenures, p. 75. Littleton, sect. 533, 534. Co. Litt., 302. (a.)

" A confirmation is of a nature nearly allied to a release." 2 Black. Com., chap. 20, pp. 325, 326.

Is there any difference between an assent that an American patent shall be issued upon a Spanish grant, and a confirmation of that grant ? What difference is there, between a confirmation of a claim, and the assent to a previous decision of the commissioners awarding a confirmation ? If Attorney General Clifford can see a difference, and distinguish and divide between confirmations of Spanish claims, and the assent by Congress to the decisions of the commissioners awarding confirmations, by providing that American patents shall issue upon them, he will have surpassed the learned Hudibras,

> " Who could distinguish and divide,
> A hair 'twixt south and southwest side ;"

And will have attained that sharpness of mental vision described by Butler,

> "It requires optics sharp, I ween,
> To see what is not to be seen."

By the second proposition, that complete Spanish grants were not confirmed, nor proposed to be confirmed, by the Congress, because they required none, as affirmed by Attorney General Clifford, it appears that his memory is as short as his understanding of a confirmation, and as treacherous as his exposition of the statutes, the law of nations, and the treaty. He asserts that, under the act of 1807, claims were confirmed ; and that certificates of confirmation had been issued under that act, and that Congress had directed patents to issue on such certificates of confirmation, (see p. 44.) Now, it turns out upon examination, that the act of 1807 was not confined to incomplete grants ; on the contrary, the provisions of that act apply clearly and comprehensively to all claims whether by complete or incomplete grants. The 4th section is so; the

5th, 7th, and 8th sections are so, without disciimination. The act of 1814, April 18, does not take section 6, to the exclusion of section 8 of the act of 1807. But sections 4 and 6 of the act of 1807 include complete French and Spanish grants in the confirmations enacted, as well as incomplete grants. Theiefore, it is erroneous to say, complete grants were not confiimed.

As to the thiid proposition, concerning the distinction taken by Attorney General Clifford between the need of incomplete Spanish titles to the protection of the United States by confirmation, which was therefore given, and the no need of the complete Spanish titles to protection, and therefore such were not confirmed, that there may be no mistake, I quote his words from page foity-seven of his printed opinion :

" The class of claims in which that of the claimants was embraced was to be reported to Congress for their final determination in pursuance of the eighth section of the act of 1807. Congress did act on these claims, as appears by the act of 12th April, 1814, and confirmed those founded on *incomplete* titles to the extent of a league square. The claims that had been biought before the board on complete and perfect titles were not confirmed, for the reason, unquestionably, that they required no confiimation fiom the Government of the United States. Such lands had been severed from the domain of the Crown of Spain before the treaty of cession, and had become private property, and were alike protected by the law of nations and by the terms of the treaty."

In this Attorney General Clifford remembers to forget that the other act of Congress, of eighteenth April, 1814, is not confined exclusively to confirmations of incomplete Spanish titles ; nor is it confined exclusively to claims not exceeding one league square, as in the act of Apiil twelfth, 1814.

If the Congress did not intend to confirm any but incomplete French and Spanish claims, by giving American patents, why pass the fourth and sixth sections of the act of 1807, and the eighth section of that same act of 1807, requiring all decisions in favor of claimants, upon complete and incomplete grants, upon claims not exceeding, and upon claims exceeding, one league squaie, to be included in the transcripts of decisions in favor of claimants, to " be laid before Congress for their final determination thereon?" If the Congress did not intend to confirm, by American patents, Spanish grants complete and perfect before the cession, whether exceeding or not exceeding one league square in extent, why enact the law of eighteenth of April, 1814, after having enacted the law of twelfth of April of that year?

The opinion, that the confirmations, approved, ordered, and sanctioned by Congress, were confined, or intended to apply, solely and exclusively, to claims brought before the board of commissioners founded "on incomplete titles to the extent of a league square," and that claims " biought before the board on complete and peifect titles weie not confirmed, is convicted of error as to matteis of fact, by the certificates of the commissioners and the acts of Congress before cited, beginning with the act of March 3d, 1805, and progressing with the successive acts to that of 18th April, 1814.

The propositions about severance from the royal domain, and the distinctions in that respect, between lands claimed by incomplete titles, and those claimed by complete and perfect titles ; and the reason for confirming the former, and not confirming the latter, founded upon the distinction, that the *incomplete* grants had not severed the lands therein described from the royal domain, had not become private property before the treaty of cession, were not protected by the law of nations and the treaty, and therefore stood in need of confirmation ; which propositions and distinctions Attorney General Clifford has put forth, are wanting in judgment, unreasonable, and convicted of error by the adjudications of the Supreme Court of the United States, so often repeated by that court, as seen in the books of reports, that it appears shameful that these propositions should have been published by the high law officer of the Government of the United States, and reported to the President of the United States whereon to institute judicial proceedings.

To that effect I cite the following cases, viz :

The United States *vs*. Delassus.   9 Peters, 132, 134, 135.

Percheman *vs*. United States.   7 Peters, 51.

United States *vs*. Sibbald.   10 Peters, 313, 321.

United States *vs*. Heirs of F. M. Arredondo, &c.   13 Peters, 133.

United States *vs*. Low.   16 Peters, 162.

United States *vs*. Clarke's heirs and Atkinson's heirs.   16 Peters, 231.

In the case of Delassus, 9 Peters, 132, the opinion of the court was delivered by Chief Justice Marshall, whose statement of the cases shows the petition of Delassus for the grant of a tract of land containing a lead mine, presented to Lieutenant Governor Trudeau in March, 1795; which petition Trudeau granted in April, 1795, by instructions to that effect from the Baron de Carondelet, governor general of Louisiana. The survey had been made, but the inchoate right had not been followed up by a complete final grant when Louisiana was delivered to the United States.   The chief justice, after commenting upon the stipulations of the first, second, and third articles of the treaty for the cession of Louisiana to the United States, proceeds to say :

" The right of property, then, is protected and secured by the treaty; and no principle is better settled in this country, than that an inchoate title to land is property.

" Independent of treaty stipulation, this right would be held sacred. The sovereign who acquires an inhabited country acquires full dominion over it ; but his dominion is never supposed to divest the vested rights of individuals to property.   The language of the treaty ceding Louisiana excludes every idea of interfering with private property ; of transferring lands which had been severed from the royal domain.   The people change their sovereign.   Their right to property remains unaffected by this change."

"In 1795, then, when these acts were performed by the lieutenant governor, under the authority and by the special order of the intendant general, those officers were the proper authorities, and had full power to make the concession, and to perfect it by a complete title.   Who can doubt that it would have been so perfected in conformity with the laws, usages, and customs of the Spanish government, had not the sovereignty in the country been transferred to the United States?"

"A grant or concession made by that officer who is by law authorized to make it, carries with it prima facie evidence that it is within his power. No excess of them, or departure from them, is to be presumed."

"This subject was fully discussed in the United States vs. Arredondo, 6 Peters, 691; Percheman vs. United States, 7 Peters, 51; and the United States vs. Clarke, 8 Peters, 436. It is unnecessary to repeat the arguments contained, the opinions given by the court in those cases."

The Supreme Court thereupon pronounced a decree, declaring the claim of the petitioner "to be valid; and doth confirm his title to the land as described in the survey made by the principal deputy surveyor of upper Louisiana on the 14th day of December, 1799, and dated the 5th March, 1800."

In the case of the United States vs. Percheman, 7 Peters, 86, 87. the same doctrine is held by the court: "The sense of justice and of right, which is acknowledged and felt by the whole civilized world, would be outraged if private property should be generally confiscated, and private rights annulled. The people change their allegiance; their allegiance to the ancient sovereign is dissolved; but their relations to each other, and their rights of property, remain undisturbed."

"A cession of territory is never understood to be a cession of property belonging to its inhabitants. The King cedes that only which belonged to him. Lands he had previously granted were not his to cede. Neither party could so understand the cession."

The cases of United States vs. Sibbald, 10 Peters, 313, 321; United States vs. the Heirs of F. M. Arredondo, &c., 13 Peters, 133; United States vs. Low, 16 Peters, 162; and the United States vs. Clarke's heirs and Atkinson's heirs, are all cases upon incomplete grants, and were adjudged to be valid, the lands having been severed from the public domain by such grants, and therefore private property, protected by the law of nations, and the treaty ceding the dominion of the country; but not disturbing private rights.

Sibbald's case was an incomplete grant, upon a condition precedent, not performed in time, nor until after the treaty of cession to the United States. Yet, in that case, the Supreme Court said: "The evidence in this and other cases, which have been decided, is very full and clear that no grant has ever been annulled or revoked by the Spanish authorities for any cause; and it may well be doubted whether it would have been reannexed to the royal domain had the province remained under the dominion of the King of Spain."

This grant, by a concession, was upon a condition to be performed, by building a mill, before the *absolute* title should vest, as expressly declared in the concession. Yet, by this concession, the lands described were severed from the royal domain, and had not been reannexed to the royal domain for non-performance of the condition. The claimant was confirmed in his title by the decree: 10 Peters, 322, 323, 325.

The distinctions attempted by the Attorney General Clifford, between incomplete grants and the complete grants, as to the severance of the lands from royal domain by the latter and non-severance by former, and as to the protection by a confirmation by the United States being necessary to claims by incomplete grants, and not so as to claims by complete and perfect grants, under the treaty for ceding Louisiana, appear by the cases cited to be without any solid foundation.

Debile fundamentum, fallit opus.

Neither has the distinction attempted between the confirmations certified under the eighth section of the act of 1807, and those certified under the sixth section of that act, so that the latter shall be "certificates of confirmation," but not the former, any better foundation. The decisions of the commissioners in favor of the claimants work the confirmations. The written evidence of such decisions, duly certified, constitute "certificates of confirmation" by the commissioners. The decisions, without the certified evidence of the decisions, can not constitute "certificates of confirmation." The several and distinct papers containing the decisions of the distinct boards of commissioners, awarding confirmations to the claimants for the lands claimed, duly signed and certified by the signatures of the commissioners, (or of a majority,) as directed by the law, constitute "certificates of confirmation," no matter who reads, who holds, who keeps them; no matter where they are deposited, whether with the Secretary of the Treasury, or in the one or the other of the halls of the Congress, or in the office of the surveyor general, or with the registers of the land offices respectively. The certificates of confirmation do not change their essence, nature, and qualities, as a Chameleon changes its color, by being placed here or there, or in the hands of this person or that.

The act of 1805, section 4, had compelled the holders of lands, by virtue of complete French or Spanish grants, to part with their grants, deeds, conveyances, or other written evidence of their claims, to be laid before the commissioners, under penalty for neglect that their title papers should not be admitted as evidence in any court of the United States against any grant derived from the United States. Moreover, the commissioners had been instructed, (in section 5 of the act of 1805,) that they should not be bound to consider a French or Spanish "grant, warrant, or order of survey," as conclusive evidence, and to inquire whether it was "antedated, or otherwise fraudulent;" and "might require such other proof of its validity as they may deem proper."

Congress having so taken from the claimants, under French and Spanish grants, complete and incomplete, the possession of their title papers, and brought them into peril and suspicion, it was but reasonable to expect that the Congress would confirm and quiet all such claimants as, upon examination, should be adjudged by the commissioners and certified to have good and valid claims under the French or Spanish laws, usages, and customs. Confirmation was intended to be made, by means of American patents, to all claimants who should be decided by the commissioners to have good and valid claims, (unless in cases wherein the Congress should think fit and proper to reverse the decisions of the commissioners.) That intention manifestly appears in the body, sense, soul, and spirit of the several acts, as well as by the forms pursued by the commissioners in awarding confirmation of every claim which they decided in favor of the claimant.

That the Congress did, by the 4th section of the act of 1807, cause the adjudications of the claimants coming within the purview of that section to work confirmations, final and conclusive, against the United States, without any further determination or act of the Congress, which entitled the claimants to have and receive patents from the United States, according to the sixth and seventh sections of that act, is so manifest that even Attorney General Clifford can not miss or gainsay the matter. The act of 1814, April 12th, is equally clear and palpable as that of 1807, in working confirmations and allowing patents to claimants, in whose favor the commissioners had decided, in cases within the purview of the statute of 12th April, 1814.

There remained a class of cases decided in favor of claimants by the commissioners, and certified in the transcripts by each of the boards of commissioners in Louisiana, viz., claims by grants, *complete* and *incomplete*, for tracts of land exceeding one league square.

The Attorney General, by his construction, confines the act of 18th April, 1814, solely to cases finally and conclusively confirmed by the act of 1807, on which patents were ordered by that same act as matters of course, and omits the second class of cases described in the act by the words "and on claims which are included in the transcripts of decisions made in favor of claimants, and transmitted to the Secretary of the Treasury," by making these words expletive, and tautologous; having no other effect than to spin out a description of claims which were exactly, fully, and identically described in the previous member of the sentence ending with the words "and which were directed to be filed with the proper register of the land office within twelve months after date."

This mode violates the rules of construction used by the sages of the law, particularly the following:

I. "A statute ought upon the whole to be so construed as that, if it can be prevented, no clause, sentence, or word shall be superfluous, void, or insignificant."—4 Bacon, ab. statute, (I.) pl. 9, p. 645.

II. "The title of a statute is not to be regarded in construing it, because this is no part of the statute."—Same book and page, placita 11; Chance *vs.* Adams, 1 Ld. Ray., 77.

The act is made and passed before the title is put to it. The title is but a name. It is impossible to comprise the whole body and enactments of statutes in their respective titles.

III. "The office of a good expositor of an act of Parliament is to make construction on all the parts together, and not of one part only by itself; nemo enim aliquam partem recte intelligere possit, antequam totum iterum atque iterum perlegerit."—Lincoln College's case, 3 Coke, 59, b.; Co. Litt., 381, a.

IV. The sages of the law in construing statutes, "have ever been guided by the intent of the legislature, which they have always taken according to the necessity of the matter, and according to that which is consonant to reason and good discretion."—Stradling *vs.* Morgan, Plowden, 205; Montjoy's case, 5 Coke, 5, a & b.; 19 Viner. statutes, (E. 6,) pl. 81, p. 519.

V. "Statutes made in pari materia are to be taken into the construction of one another. An act lately made shall be taken within the equity of an act made long since."—Viner. supra, pl. 109, p. 523; Vernon's case, 4 Coke, 4, a & b.

VI. "When a particular thing is enacted, given, or limited in the preceding part of a statute, this shall not be altered or taken away by any subsequent general words of the same statute."—Standon *vs.* University of Oxon and Whitton, 1 Jon., 26; IV Bacon, ab. statute, (I.) pl. 17, p. 645; XIX Viner. statutes, (E. 6,) pl. 110, page 523.

The Attorney General makes the whole act, in its body and effect, to operate nothing more than what had been amply and particularly provided for by the 4th, 6th, and 7th sections of the act of March 3, 1807.

This act of 1807, in section 4, 6, and 7, had finally confirmed one class of claims coming within the purview of the fourth section of that act, and had provided the means by which those claimants might obtain American patents.

The act of 12th April, 1814, had confirmed finally another class of claims, which had been subject to the review of Congress over the decisions of the commissioners, and the means were provided by which those claimants could obtain American patents.

A third class remained of decisions of the commissioners in favor of claimants, subject to the final determination of the Congress thereon. The moral obligation binding the Congress to confirm finally and quiet those claimants, was of a character as high and as imperative as the faith due to the treaty of cession, (considering the circumstances in which the Congress had placed them by the several acts before mentioned,) and equipollent with those considerations of equity, justice, and good discretion which had influenced the confirmations finally given to the two former classes by the before mentioned acts of 1807, sections 4, 6, and 7, and of 12th April, 1814. By the act of 18th April, 1814, the Congress discharged their duty by including this third class of claimants in that act by the words, "and on claims which are included in the transcript of decisions made in favor of claimants, and transmitted to the Secretary of the Treasury." This description was clear, accurate, and true, applicable to that class of claimants, and the only remaining class for which the Congress had not then provided the means of quiet by obtaining American patents—the only class remaining for the determination of Congress on the decisions of the commissioners. According to the necessity of the matter, according to good discretion and equity, the Congress were bound to act and to determine on those decisions in favor of claimants included in the transcripts then before the Congress. They acted and determined thereon, and included them in the means provided for obtaining American patents.

These claimants being so included in a preceding part of the statute, shall not be excluded "by any general words of the same statute" The words and clause which includes them must have effect in the construction of the statute. Those words cannot be rendered "superfluous, void, or insignificant."

The Attorney General Clifford, to exclude this third class of claimants by grants complete and grants incomplete, for tracts of land exceeding one league square, included in the certified transcripts made by the two boards respectively of their decisions in favor of claimants, would make the Congress do an act which their duty did not require, and render the whole act of 18th April, 1814, nothing more than a repetition of that which they had substantially and efficiently enacted in the 4th, 6th, and 7th sections of the act of 1807, (then in full force, and not limited in its duration,) to the total neglect of their duty and good faith towards a class of claimants equally entitled to the consideration of the Congress, as that class to which he would confine the act as being nothing more than a duplicated confirmation.

In the constructions of the acts of Congress, and expositions of the Spanish grant, the law of nations, and the treaty, Attorney General Clifford sticks in the surface. It cannot be said, bæret in cortice, for he has not penetrated so far as the bark; bæret in muscus corticis—he has entangled himself in the moss of the bark, there buzzed like a fly in a cobweb, and imagined distinctions where no differences exist, to the end to make the thirteenth Congress do that which they had no need to do, and leave undone that which in duty and good faith they were bound to have done.

III. *Length of time and non claim.*

The possession of Spain continued, in fact, for upwards of twenty-seven years after this grant, before the jurisdiction was transferred to the United States; during all which time the Spanish authority made no grant within the boundaries of the grant to Conway, which extended to the Amite and Lake Maurepas; and, with knowledge that it was so claimed, held, and possessed, made the governmental sale and conveyance of part to Faure, for public dues assessed against the owner.

On the third day of March, 1806, the commissioners appointed under the acts of Congress before mentioned decided upon the claims respectively made by Conway, (commissioners' certificate No. 125,) by Daniel Clark, (certificate No. 127,) and on the 10th of March, 1806, in the case of Donaldson *vs.* Scott, (commissioners' certificate No. 133,) all claiming under the grant to Maurice Conway, "with depth to the river Amite," and confirmed those claims respectively.

In March, 1806, the authorities of the United States had notice, not only by the actual possession of the claimants, but by this proceeding before the commissioners, of the extent of this grant   Moreover, in the first volume of the Laws of the United States, published by **Bioren &** **Duane**, by authority of an act of Congress, (pp. 551 to 554,) this claim, by the petition of Conway to the governor general, the order of survey, the report thereon, and the complete grant of the Governor General Galvez, are set out, with the note that the parties claim this grant as running back to the river Iberville, Amite, and the Lake Maurepas.   Thus for more than forty years the Government of the United States have acquiesced also.   No proceeding has been instituted, during all that time, to divest the claimants of their possessions under this Spanish grant.   Before the commissioners the claim was so distinctly presented by the grant and conveyances, and by a plat, and the commissioners decided in favor of the claimants to the extent claimed, and confirmed the claims as good and valid.

Two generations and more have passed away, seventy years and more have rolled around, since the grant by the Spanish governor and intendant general of Louisiana was made to Maurice Conway; during which time he and his alienees, and their descendants and assigns, have held the possession, undisturbed by any action, bill, plaint, or inquest of office, save only by the proceedings before the special commission instituted by Congress by the before mentioned acts of 1805, 1806, and 1807, in which the commissioners decided in favor of the claimants, and confirmed their claims.

The duty of Congress to maintain and protect the private rights and interests of land which had originated before the cession of Louisiana to the United States, and to secure the free enjoyment thereof by the proprietors, was imperative by the law of nations and the express stipulations of the treaty.   The duty of Congress, to ascertain the public domain, and to put the public lands into market to pay the purchase of Louisiana, thereby to relieve the people from the burthen of the purchase, as far as could be reasonably effected by sales of the purchased public lands, was likewise clear.   That the acts of 1805, 1806, 1807, 1811, and 1814, were intended to observe and fulfil the twofold duties of the Congress to the claimants of private rights and interests to lands in the ceded territory, originated before the cession, and deemed sacred by the law of nations and the express stipulations of the treaty, and to the citizens of the United States generally in relation to the public domain, cannot be doubted upon the reading of those acts.   To ascertain the private rights and interests, and to respect them, and thereby to ascertain the public lands and to put them to sale, are twin motives and intentions manifested in those statutes.   Public faith, the law of nations, and the treaty, secured all private rights and interests of lands in the ceded territory from sale by the United States.   Public lands, public property only, was ceded to the United States.   Private rights and interests were not ceded; to such lands the United States acquired no title, could convey none; and sales of such by the United States would have been null, avoided by the treaty, impotent according to the law of nations and the treaty.   The United States could not in good faith sell to citizens, and receive their money for lands to which they could no assure a title to the purchasers. They could not assure good titles to purchasers, until the public lands acquired by the cession were ascertained and separated from the private rights and interests in the territory ceded.

To observe good faith, as well to the claimants whose private rights and interests were to remain valid and secure under the treaty of cession, as also to those who should purchase lands in the ceded territory, was the whole principle involved in the appointment of the boards of commissioners to ascertain and determine the rights of claimants.

As Congress had reserved to themselves the right to determine finally upon the claims adjudged and certified by the commissioners to be good and valid; and as the Congress, after the commissioners had adjudged numerous claims in favor of claimants as good and valid; and after Congress had, on March 3d, 1811, expressly prohibited the officers of Government from offering for sale any of the lands, the claims to which had been laid before commissioners, "till after the final decision of Congress thereon;" it cannot admit of a doubt that Congress did intend, and were under duties of the highest moral obligation, to determine, CYPRES, finally, upon the transcripts of decisions made by the commissioners in favor of claimants, when the transcripts, duly certified by commissioners, were laid before the Congress for that purpose, as the laws had directed.

In January, 1812, those transcripts of decisions in favor of claimants were laid before the Congress, duly certified by the commissioners. In 1814, the Congress took up those transcripts, and passed the two acts of 12th and 18th April, 1814, not reversing any decision of the commissioners in favor of claimants, but providing for patents to issue upon them. From January, 1812, when these transcripts were laid before the Congress, to April, 1814, the Congress had ample time to examine the decisions in favor of claimants, and to come to their determination. They passed the acts of 1814, the one on the 12th, the other on the 18th April. From that time forward the Congress have not passed any other determination upon those transcripts of decisions in favor of those claimants. Thirty-three years have elapsed since those determinations were made by the Congress. No other notice by Congress has been taken of those decisions in favor of claimants. The provision contained in the 10th section of the act of March 3d, 1811, has during all that time stood unrepealed, operating to prohibit any sales by the United States of any of the lands contained in the decisions of the commissioners in favor of claimants, until after the determination of Congress thereon.

This great length of time since the acts of 12th and 18th April, 1814, without any further notice taken by Congress of those transcripts of decisions in favor of claimants, is presumptive evidence, presumption violent, of the construction given by the Congress to those two statutes, as confirming all those decisions in favor of claimants contained in the transcripts so laid before the Congress for their determination. In that sense and meaning of those statutes, the thirteenth Congress discharged their obligations of duty to the nation and to those claimants. But upon the construction given by Attorney General Clifford, that the class of cases, including all the claims exceeding one league square, decided in favor of claimants by the commissioners, are omitted, and not confirmed by the Congress by their act of 18th April, 1814, then the thirteenth Congress, and sixteen others, filling a space of thirty-four years, were guilty of neglect of their duty to determine upon that class of claims.

Taking the act of March 3d, 1811, passed about five years after the commissioners had confirmed these claims, of Conway, (certificate No. 125,) Daniel Clark, (certificate No. 128,) and Donaldson & Scott, (No. 133,) (as extending in depth to the Amite, Iberville, or Maurepas;) and the acts of 12th and of 18th April, 1814, together, in pari materia, the conclusion is fair and inevitable that the true intent and meaning of the thirteenth Congress, as expressed in their said acts of 12th and 18th April, 1814, was a confirmation of all the claims decided in favor of the claimants, then certified by the commissioners to the Secretary of the Treasury, and by him laid before the Congress for their determination. The construction of Attorney General Clifford, involving the Congress in such dereliction of their duty during such great length of time, is not fair, not reasonable, not just, not equitable.

Attorney General Clifford says, (page 39,) "this claim has not been recognised by the Executive department. It had been steadily resisted, by the General Land Office, from the first moment when it was presented to Mr. Graham, in 1829, and never received the sanction of the head of that bureau."

This argument may seem very imposing to men who hold that the Executive department alone is the Government, that the Executive can do no wrong, and that non-resistance and passive obedience are due to Executive will. But the opinion and report of the Attorney General had relation to the question whether or not proceedings should be instituted to invoke a determination by the Judiciary at the instance of the United States; therefore his attention was due to the principles decided by the courts of justice bearing on these cases, arising under Spanish grants and the treaty of cession of Louisiana to the United States, to the adjudications of the Supreme Court of the United States in like cases— not to what the head of an Executive bureau had done upon the subject. To those who know that the tenures of private rights and interests of lands do not hang by Executive will, but are under the protection of the Judiciary, and who know that the predetermination of the officers of the Executive departments in Washington (with a few honorable exceptions) is to decide every claim against the citizen, if doubts and technicalities and finical objections can be raised to stifle conscience, this argument, drawn from the actings in the Land Office, will appear frothy, and unbecoming a high law officer of the Government of the United States.

If the Executive discretion and authority was so potential in this matter, why sleep for forty-live years from the cession of Louisiana, for forty-two years after the decisions of the commissioners in favor of the claimants, and for thirty-three years after the Congress had deliberated and made their determination upon the transcripts of decisions in favor of claimants, laid before the Congress specially and by direction of law for their determination? Why did not the Executive institute proceedings at law to evict these intruders upon the public domain—upon these lands in the rear of the forty-two arpens in depth? Why did not the Executive remove such intruders by military force?

Sufficient answer to such acquiescence, in what Attorney General Clifford now supposes to be intrusion, is to be found in this, these claimants were no intruders upon the public domain of the United States. Maurice Conway, and his heirs, alienees, and those claiming under his title, have public legal evidence of possession, delivered in 1776, by decree and order of Onzaga, the governor general of Louisiana, followed by the complete grant of Governor General Galvez; held thenceforward under the Government of Spain for about twenty-seven years, under sanction of the constituted authorities of Spain, manifesting a severance of those lands from the royal domain of Spain, whereby these lands had become private property, secured and protected by the law of nations and the treaty ceding the dominion of the country to the United States; which possession and title was confirmed by the board of commissioners in 1806, certified by them to the Congress, and approved by them in April, 1814, and ever thereafter acquiesced in by the Congress of the United States.

The possession and enjoyment of Maurice Conway, and those claiming and holding from and under him, has now been continued for more than seventy years.

The courts, by the proceedings to be instituted, are to sit in judgment upon transactions of great antiquity, after all the original parties are dead, after the memory of witnesses has faded, (if indeed any who lived in that day and place survive.) The claimants must pay their own costs, although they prevail against the United States, for no costs can be adjudged against the United States for false clamor; and. lastly, the odious doctrine of nullum tempus occurrit regi, is to be insisted on as being of the very essence of the proceeding—indispensably necessary to give color of right to maintain the demand; for, if the positive bar by statutable limitation to suits and remedies would apply, the Government would be without hope.

How far this royal prerogative exemption from the effect of the statutes of limitation (unless the King be by special words comprehended) ought to be allowed in the United States, considering the spirit and fundamental principles of the American Government, in contrast with the spirit and foundations of Kingly governments, and those unnatural and false positions which acknowledge the King as the owner of *his* government, *his* parliament, and his *people*, personally irresponsible to the law, incapable of wrong, and sacred as the Divinity, is a question never solemnly argued in the United States, although worthy of the most serious discussion.

That question I shall not discuss here. I know it has been taken for granted in the States, and likewise in the Supreme Court of the United States, without solemn argument at bar. The time may come when another Hampden or another Sidney may find it necessary, because of excessive abuse, to arouse the nation to a sense of true constitutional principles upon this subject.

In this case the discussion of that question is unnecessary, because the treaty is the act of two sovereign parties, and the supreme law of the land. That treaty, and the law of nations, will be the rule of decision so long as the sacred faith of treaties is respected; which cannot be disrespected without undermining all the security which princes and States have with respect to each other.

The mover of the resolution, directed to the Attorney General, has skimmed the surface.

Suppose the American patent repealed, or that it had never been issued. What then? Are the claimants unprotected because this outward defence, superadded by the act of 18th April, 1814, has been taken from them? Not at all. The petition to Onzaga, his concession thereon, the survey by Andry, and the final grant by Galvez, remain; the contemporaneous construction of that grant, and the acquiescence of the Spanish authorities for twenty-seven years, remain; the treaty of cession remains; the law of nations remains; the faith of treaties remains; the integrity of the Supreme Court remains; and the reports of their decisions remain. The question of the validity of the title of the claimants to these lands under the Spanish grant, knit to a possession of more than seventy years, will not depend upon what the head of a bureau in the American Land Office thought about the propriety of resisting the application for an American patent in confirmation of the Spanish grant. The questions will be upon the effect of the Spanish grant; the effect of the claim, and possession under it during all the time from the survey of Andry, of October, 1776, and grant of Galvez, in June, 1777, to the treaty of cession to the United States, signed on the 30th April, 1803, and to the time of the change of flags in the ceded country; upon what the American Government could and could not rightfully do, and has done, in relation to the private possession so held under the laws, usages, and customs of Spain; the Spanish order of survey and grant, together with the exposition of that grant made by the Spanish authorities themselves whilst the sovereignty of the country belonged to the Spanish Crown; and, finally, upon the effect of the claim of title and possession under it to the Amite and the lake, during the whole time from 1776 to 1848, without let, hindrance, or suit against the possessors and claimants.

If these lands were severed from the public domain under the Spanish government, and never were reannexed during the sovereignty and jurisdiction of Spain, then under the treaty of St. Ildefonso, between Spain and France, and the treaty of cession between France and the United States, the true meaning of the first, second, and third articles of the treaty of cession to the United States will protect the private rights of these claimants against the claim and demand of the United States.

The grant of Galvez to Conway, the construction given to it by the authorities of Spain, the exposition of the grant made by the advertisement, sale, and conveyance to Faure by the Government of Spain for the public dues in arrear from the estate of St. Maxent, holding under the grant to Conway, are evidences irresistible to show that the lands granted to Conway were not limited to forty-two arpens in depth, but extended as far as the Amite and the lake, without prejudice to any person having a previous grant. The acquiescence of all the authorities of Spain, the absence of any conflicting grant made by the Spanish government, or any officer thereof, during all the succeeding years of Spanish sovereignty, prove the construction and effect of that grant to Conway, as severing the lands from the public domain of Spain, within the given courses, extended to the river Amite and Lake Maurepas.

As to the possession in the rear of the forty-two arpens in depth, and exceeding the additional two arpens, (to which the Attorney General would limit the grant of Galvez,) extending to the Amite and the lake, to which the commissioners, by their decisions, confirmed the claims, the whole length of possession has now exceeded seventy-two years, before the judicial proceeding, ordered by the President, has been instituted. But the doctrine of nullum tempus occurrit regi, is to be relied on by the United States.

There is a difference between a positive and conclusive bar by a plea of the statute of limitations, and presumption from length of time, used by way of evidence. By the first, the Government may not be bound, (in the general.) By the latter, presumptive evidence, from length of time, the Government is bound. Prescription and usucaption apply between nation and nation, and between a nation and its subjects and citizens.

The difference between length of time which is to operate as a peremptory bar to a claim, and length of time which is only used by way of evidence, is this, courts and juries are bound and concluded by length of time prescribed by statute and pleaded in bar to a claim though they may be satisfied that the demand is just, it is still a bar; but length of time, used merely by way of evidence, leaves the court and jury to inferences of other facts, to presume all to have been solemnly done which is necessary to the perfection of the thing under which ancient and long continued use and possession has been enjoyed.

This distinction is clearly taken and explained by Lord Mansfield, in Mayor of Kingston-upon-Hull vs. Horner, 1 Cowper, 108, 109, and acted upon in these cases:

Powell vs. Milbanke: 1 Cowp., 103, in note.

Rex vs. Carpenter: 2 Shower, 47.

Lord Purbeck's case: 1 Cowp., 109.

The King vs. Brown: 1 Cowp., 110.

Bedle vs. Beard: 12 Co , 5, 6.

Jones vs. Turbeville: 2 Vez., jun., 11, 15.

Pickering *vs.* Stamford: 2 Vez., jun., 583.
Archer *vs.* Sadler: 2 Hen. and Munf., 376, 377.
Holcroft *vs.* Heal: 1 Bos. and Pulleb, 401.

These cases explain the doctrine of presumption from length of time to maintain and make good ancient possessions, by presuming a grant from the King, letters patent, or whatever is necessary. They show that the King himself is not excepted. Examples are there given where the grants produced, supposed to have given the thing possessed, were found to be insufficient; and even containing an express exception, the party has been allowed to abandon that, and rely upon length of time, as presumptive evidence, that there was another grant sufficient to sustain the possession. These presumptions are indulged by juries, judges, and chancellors, in cases within their respective and appropriate spheres.

In Bedle and others *vs.* Beard, (2 Co., 5,) the grant produced by the plaintiffs, to maintain their right, was adjudged insufficient to grant the rectory; "yet, it was resolved by Lord Chancellor Ellesmere, with the principal judges, and upon consideration of the precedents, it shall now be intended, in respect of the ancient and continual possession, that there was a lawful grant of the King. Omnia præsumuntur solemniter esse acta—all shall be presumed to be done which might make the ancient appropriation good; for tempus est ædax rerum, and records, and letters patent, and other writings, either consume, or are lost and embezzled; and God forbid that ancient grants and acts should be drawn in question, although they can not now be shown, which were at first necessary to the perfection of the thing; which, if drawn in question in the lifetime of any of the parties to it, they might have shown the truth of the matter. If any exception or objection should now prevail, the ancient and long possession would hurt, instead of strengthen, the title."

In the case of Rex *vs.* Brown, (Cowper, 110,) the evidence of the title of the defendant was a possession and enjoyment of one hundred years ; and Lord Mansfield held " that though such possession and enjoyment should not conclude as a positive bar, because there was no statute of limitations against the Crown, yet it might operate as evidence against the Crown of right in the defendant, though the commencement could not be shown."

In the case of Millebanke and Powell, (reported in note, Cowper, 103) Upon two presentations and enjoyment by the two incumbents from 1694 to 1769, a period of seventy-five years, Lord Mansfield left these two nominations and enjoyment of those incumbents for seventy-five years under the Hedworth family as evidence to the jury from which to presume another grant from the Crown of the curacy, (which was excepted out of the grant produced,) to the Hedworth family, under which the presentment of Millebanke was made in opposition to the presentment of Powell made by the Crown. The jury presumed a grant, and found a verdict accordingly.

This presumption applies between nations ; between a prince and his subjects or citizens ; between subject and subject, citizen and citizen.

It belongs to the law of nations, and to the municipal code of every people. It is not a hard, dry, technical rule ; but is founded in nature, in ethics, in reason and experience, as many illustrious men have said and proved.

Grotius de jure, belli et pacis, book 2, chap. 4.

Wolfius, Jus. Nat., part 3.

Pufendorf, Jus. Nat. and Gent., part 10.

Vattel, book 2, chap. XI, p. 174 to 178.

Hillary vs. Waller.   12 Vez., pp. 239, 264, 266.

Smith vs. Clay, (in note to Deloraine vs. Browne.)   3 Brown, Ch. Rep., p. 639.

In the case of Hillary vs. Waller, Lord Chancellor Erskine elegantly and clearly explains the true reason and philosophy of the doctrine of presumption.

" The presumption in courts of law from length of time stands upon a clear principle, built upon reason, the nature and character of man, and the result of human experience.   It resolves itself into this, that a man will naturally enjoy what belongs to him.   That is the whole principle."   " As to a bond taken, and no interest paid for twenty years ; nay, within twenty years, as Lord Mansfield has said, but upon twenty years the presumption is that it has been paid, and the presumption will hold, unless it can be repelled ; unless insolvency—or absence, &c., be shown ; or something which repels the presumption that a man is always ready to enjoy his own.   The case of a mortgage is an instance.   I remember a case before Lord Mansfield.   A mortgagee brought his ejectment ; the deeds proved, accompanied with the bond, all went for nothing ; he had not received, for twenty-five years, though living in a street with the mortgagor, any money upon the mortgage ; and upon that the mortgage was considered satisfied.   It has been said you can not presume unless you believe.   Mankind, from the infirmity and necessity of their situation, must for the preservation of their property and rights have recourse to some general principle, to take the place of individual and specific belief, which can only hold as to matters within our own time."   " Therefore, upon the weakness and infirmity of all human tribunals, judging of matters of antiquity, instead of belief, which must be founded on the judgment upon a recent transaction, the legal presumption (in matters of antiquity) holds the place of particular and individual belief."

If granted that the United States are not bound by the statute of limitations, because " nullum tempus occurrit regi," and the statute can not be pleaded as a positive bar, yet they are bound by evidence ; and length of possession is evidence, to operate, in matters of antiquity, as a legal foundation for presuming " all to have been solemnly done which was necessary to perfect the thing."   Foreign laws, usages, and customs are matters of evidence ; of such, our courts cannot take judicial notice; they must be proved.   The meaning of Spanish words, phrases, technical terms, and peculiar modes of speech, translated into the English language, are matters of evidence, matters of proof.

The meaning and effect of the survey and grant made and done in the years 1776 and 1777, written in the Spanish tongue, and executed by Spanish officers during the time when Spain had the domain and sovereignty of the country, whereby a possession of the lands claimed has been held and continued for upwards of seventy years, commencing under the Crown of Spain, and continued under the Republic of France; and during forty-eight years under the land-coveting people of the United States, are, all in all, matters of evidence, to lay a foundation for presuming " all to have been solemnly done which were necessary to perfect the thing."

In questions of this kind there is no positive rule which says twenty, thirty, fifty, seventy, or an hundred years, or any other length of time, shall be sufficient ground to presume a charter, or " whatever is necessary to perfect the thing." (Mayor of Hull vs. Horner. Cowper, 110.) The presumption depends upon the circumstances and the nature of the thing.

The Attorney General Clifford has thought fit to say, (page 7 of his printed opinion,) " It is much to be regretted, that the figurative plan or sketch referred to by Andry, and which he delivered to Conway, had not been preserved, or, if still in existence, that it had not been produced as a part of the evidence in the case."

That it was not preserved and delivered to the Attorney General in 1847, (after a lapse of seventy years and more,) is a muckle pity. But Conway was dead, Clarke was dead, St. Maxent was dead, Donaldson and Scott were dead, Wade Hampton was dead, Galvez was dead; two generations and more had passed, and what had become of that figurative plan or sketch? Who last had it, or who was entitled to have it, or who had the keeping of it, are mysteries obscured and buried in the grave of things past. Conway, it is to be presumed, delivered it to the governor and intendant general, Galvez, by whose order it was made and reported, whereby and whereon to found a complete grant. Did Galvez send it to the public office where the petition of Conway, Onzaga's decree thereon, Andry's process verbal and report to Galvez, and his final grant to Conway, were all deposited for record? In the language of Lord Chancellor Ellesmere, "tempus est ædax rerum, and records, and letters patent, and other writings, are either consumed, or are lost, or embezzled; and God forbid that ancient grants and acts should be called in question, although they cannot be shewn, which, if they had been drawn in question in the lifetime of any of the parties, they might have shewn the truth of the matter."

If the figurative plan or sketch originally made by Andry (that is to to say, the diagram or plat) could be produced, and should exhibit to the eye the lines N. 50° W. and S. 70° E., without a closing line at the depth of forty-two arpens, drawn from the one post to the other, but showing an extension beyond the two stakes, and the depth left open, then the Attorney General Clifford would be satisfied that the grant was not limited in depth to the two additional arpens, but continued on following the same courses.

The public records and papers passed, by the cession of Louisiana, from the custody of Spanish officers to the keeping of the officers of the United States; and now, after seventy odd years, and the death of all the original parties to the transactions, this original figurative plan, made by Andry, cannot be produced. Under such circumstances, in judging of matters of such antiquity, mankind, from the infirmity and necessity of their situation, for the preservation of their property and rights, have recourse to some general principle, to supply the place of those writings, and papers, and witnesses, which time, in its eating, destroying course, has swept away. That general principle, which the law has adopted in such cases, is presumption; and the established doctrine of law and equity is, all shall be presumed which at first was necessary to the perfection of the thing, rather than to draw in question ancient grants and acts, to impeach them after so many successions of years, and after the death of all the parties. Such is the doctrine of Lord Chancellor Ellesmere. and the principal judges, in Bedle *vs.* Beard, 12 Co. 5; of Lord Mansfield, in Mayor of Kingston-upon-Hull *vs.* Horner, Cowper, 102; of the Lord Commissioners Eyre and Ashhurst, in Jones *vs.* Turbeville, 2 Vez., jr., 13; of Sir Richard Pepper Arden, master of the rolls, in Pickering *vs.* Stamford, 2 Vez., jr., 583; of Lord Chancellor Eldon, in O'Connor *vs.* Cook, 6 Vez., jr., 673, 674; and of Lord Chancellor Erskine, in Hillary *vs.* Waller, 12 Vez., 265, 267; and of various other chancellors and judges.

The presumption that Andry's figurative plan, or diagram, did exbibit the side lines extended beyond the distance of forty-two arpens, and as not closed by a line from one of those posts to the other, is violent and irresistible when we look at that which is not lost—at that which Andry was ordered to do; when we take his own certificate of his operations; the words of Governor Galvez, in his grant founded on it; the actings of the Spanish authorities after it; and the continual possession held by the grantee and those claiming under him. In our American usage, surveyors make a plat or figure of the land, and write the courses, and distances, and abuttals, on the same paper; this paper is called a plat and certificate of survey; the plat and certificate are both recorded in the surveyor's office; the original plat and certificate of survey is deposited in the General Land Office, there filed, and a grant of the Government issues, containing a copy of the certificate of survey, but not a copy of the plat. In conveyances the bearings, and distances, and abuttals are usually given; but not the diagram. Such is the American usage. So that the original plat and certificate may be had by resorting to the surveyor's office, or to the General Land Office, if the destroyer, time, shall not have swept away both of these.

Yet any geometrician, or any other person who knows the use of Gunter's scale and dividers, having the bearings and descriptions contained in the grant or deed of conveyance, can protract a diagram or figurative plan of the land described.

So, from the original records of the writings which are preserved—consisting of the memorial and petition of Maurice Conway to his excelleney Onzaga; his decree, and order to Andry, thereon; Andry's certificate of his operations, returned to his excellency Galvez; and his recital of the previous proceedings, and the words of the final grant thereon—any geometrician or practical man, knowing the use of the protractor and dividers, can protract a figurative plan or sketch, to supply the loss which Attorney General Clifford so deeply deplores, and desired to see. And it may be confidently affirmed that no geometrician or mathematician, in protracting a figurative plan, sketch, or diagram of the grant made by his excellency Galvez, would close the grant at the distance of forty-two arpens from the river Mississippi, as being all the land petitioned for, conceded by Onzaga, and finally granted, in the name of the King, by Galvez. No discreet geometrician or mathematician, upon inspecting the writings, would think of closing the survey by a back line from the one post on the one line at forty-two arpens from the river, to the other post on the other line at the same distance from the river, thereby to confine the additional grant of 21st June, 1777, to the depth of only two additional arpens. Such would be in flat contradiction to the writings and title papers.

The memorial of Maurice Conway to his excellency Onzaga, in the Spanish language, refers to his possession of the land purchased:.

"De los Indios Houmas," confirmed by his excellency Onzaga, in 1774, as being in depth only forty arpens; by which shortness of depth I cannot reach nor possess "los cipres necessarios a la formacion de mis barreras y demas utilidades de una habitacion," (the cypress trees so necessary for enclosures, and other utilities of a habitation;) which shortness of depth of forty arpens (not quite a mile and a half of English measure) fell short of the cypress trees, which were distant "una legua y media del rio," (a league and a half from the river, that is of four and a half miles from the river, the old French league being equal to five thousand three hundred and twenty-eight yards of English measure;) therefore the memorial prayed his excellency to take into consideration the circumstances, and to grant the petitioner "todo el fondo que hubiere vacante tras o al cabo de los suso dicho quarenta arpanes de fondo," ("all and in depth which may pass as disengaged behind or at the end of the aforesaid forty arpens in depth.")

So was the memorial of the necessity which the petitioner was under to have the cypress timber for enclosures and other utilities for his habitation. Upon this Onzaga decreed and ordered Andry to go to the land mentioned in the memorial, " Y dara posesion al suplicante de la que hubiere vacante despues de los quarenta arpanes de profundidad que posee, siguiendo la misma division, estando vacante y no causando perjuicio a los circunvecinos"—(" and give possession to the petitioner of that which may pass as disengaged after the forty arpens in depth which he possesses, pursuing the same division or course, being vacant and not causing injury to the neighbors or adjacents.")

Under this authority and order Andry, (not the surveyor but a military officer specially selected for the occasion,) certifies his operations: that he went on the land ; first ascertained the precise locality of the first forty arpens in depth by ninety-six arpens in front purchased of the Houmas and Bayou Goulas Indians, by calling together the commandant of the district and the Indian chief, and the neighbors Francis Duhon and M. Chiasson, the adjacent proprietors, to show their boundaries, finding thereby the same stakes which he had planted in 1773, for the boundary of that tract of land, having its upper and lower corners on the river, and the course of the upper line north 50 west with Duhon, and of the lower line south 70 east with Chiasson. The front he measured and reports at ninety-six arpens on the river, opening one hundred and twenty degrees towards the depth. This Andry certifies he did, " tirando a este efecto por el monte las lineas precisas, para cerciorarme de su extencion,"—" drawing to this effect through the woods the precise lines, to assure myself of his enlargement."

The lines thus spoken of are those which define the front and depth of ninety-six arpens by forty arpens ; the upper line north 50 west, the lower line north 70 east.

Having fixed the foundation, Andry says, " procedi a pone el pretendiente en posesion de la profundidad que por el antecedente decreto se le otorga ;" " I proceeded to put the petitioner in possession of the depth which by the aforementioned decree belonged to him." The manner of so giving the possession is detailed by Andry, he pointed out the upper boundary joining Duhon, the old muniments on that line, and also placed others upon that line in different places. These Andry calls " terminos," landmarks, to show the course so as to pursue the direction; ("termino" and lindero" are both Spanish words, signifying "landmarks," not *corners*, and are so used by Andry;) but did not place any one stake or post as a corner, as the utmost verge of the possession given. Every stake set in a line, every tree marked along a line as a fore and aft tree, or chopped on the right or the left side of the line, to render it visible, is a landmark; but every landmark, or " termino," every marked tree, or post, or stake, is not a corner whereat to stop one course and pursue a different course. Having traced and shown to Maurice Conway and the attendants this upper line, and planted stakes along it, Andry went on the lower line at the river, and ran with Chiasson N. 70 east, and placed stakes along that to the distance of forty-two arpens from the river, where he placed another stake, not as a corner to terminate the depth of the possession he gave to the petitioner in pursuance of the decree. Having on that line planted various posts which he calls "terminos," landmarks, or singly "termino," landmark, he placed, at the distance of 42 arpens from the river, "del mismo termino que el antecedente, para no deviar el rumbo," not as corner from whence to change the direction, and run to the former post at 42 arpens on the upper line, but "para no deviar el rumbo," in order not to deviate from the point of the compass."

Upon the report made by Andry to his excellency Galvez, the final grant was given, which alludes to the petition to the decree of Onzaga thereon, to Andry's operations thereunder, by which he had given possession to "Don Mauricio Conway en virtud del decreto antecedente, de toda la tierra vacante y detras ó á lo espalda de los primeros que posee sobre noventa y seis arpanes de trente a rio. Siguiendo la misma direccion de estos"—"the possession of all the land vacant and behind, or at the back part of the forty which he first possessed, by ninety-six arpens in front on the river, pursuing the same direction of these." Having so recited the possession given to Conway, Galvez then approves and grants to Conway the aforesaid lands behind or at the end of the forty arpens which contain his habitation, in the district of Lafourche, by ninety-six arpens in front on the river, "siguiendo la misma direccion que corre aquellos"—"pursuing the same direction which those run."

Upon these documents common sense revolts against the idea of closing the additional grant by a line from one stake to the other, at forty-two arpens only from the river; the documents give no direction for such a line; no course is given from the one to the other; Andry never run nor proposed such a line, nor limits the depth to forty-two arpens, but leaves the depth not limited. The petition and decree contemplated an extent not less than a league and a half, equal to seven thousand nine hundred and ninety-two yards of English measure, to reach and then include the cypress trees, instead of stopping short at forty-two arpens from the river, equal to two thousand seven hundred and thirty yards only of English measure, and thereby to give the pitiful addition of but two arpens in depth, equal to about one hundred and fifty yards of our measure.

The presumption is violent and irresistible, that the figurative plan or plat, made by Andry, exhibited the front on the river Mississippi, of ninety-six arpens, opening in the rear, shewing the respective courses to the depth of forty arpens as the old grant, and the same courses continued by forty-two arpens, and continuing on in the rear of those, showing the fork within which, indefinitely running, M. Conway had the right and possession over and above his former front and depth; and that there was no line to close the survey at the depth of forty-two arpens from the river. Conway would have accepted no such survey; Andry proposed no such. It would have been contrary to the petition and concession under which Andry proceeded. It is contrary to the words, sense, and meaning of the complete grant given by Galvez.

According to principles established by chancellors, and judges, and juries in the cases cited, when applied to the facts and circumstances appearing in the documents quoted by the Attorney General Clifford, and to the length of time and continual possession, every thing should be presumed in favor of the claimants; but the Attorney General has presumed every thing against them, every thing in favor of those who have slept upon their demands for more than seventy years, every thing in favor of those who have shown nothing at all "which repels the presumption that a man is always ready to enjoy what is his own."

Looking at the treaty of cession of Louisiana to the United States, the decisions of the commissioners in 1806, the doings of the Congress upon the transcripts of the decisions in favor of the claimants, the pos-session delivered by Andry to Conway, in 1776, the final grant in 1777, the terms of the petition, concession, and final grant, the intent and meaning arising fairly upon the terms of the grant, the construction given to it by the Spanish authorities before the cession of Louisiana, and the decisions of the Supreme Court in the cases before cited, in connexion with the length of possession, and non claim by Spain, France, and the United States, and comparing these with the opinion and report of Attorney General Clifford to the President, that report seems to be "monstrum horrendum, forma ingens, cui lumen ademptum." The character and spirit of the Executive of the United States, in ordering proceedings to claim for the United States the lands in the rear of the first forty-two arpens in depth, by ninety-six arpens in front, the terms of the treaty notwithstanding, viewed in comparison with the conduct of the Spanish authorities towards the claimants under this Spanish grant, is Punic faith in contrast with pure Castilian honor.

The adjudged cases, the principles well established by multiplied precedents, ought to have warned the Attorney General of the United States that the courts of justice, in adjudicating upon matters drawing in question grants and acts of such great antiquity, followed by ancient and continual possession, will not require the possessors to produce a paper title drawn up so formally, nicely, amply, exactly, critically, comprehensively, strictly, and legally, as if it had been penned by that great scrivener and erudite scholar, described by Chaucer,

> "He could then write endite, and maken a thing,
> And there was no wight could pinch at his writing."

So far from requiring a paper-title penned with such strict, legal acumen, the judges will consider of the Spanish laws, usages, and customs, the phrases and idioms used in Spanish grants, the law of nations, the treaty, and the acts of Congress applicable to the case, and apply them to the ancient grants and acts, and continual possession, in a spirit of justice, equity, and good faith; they will conform their judgments to the maxim, "Omnia presumuntur solemniter esse acta;" and after the death of all the parties to the original transactions, and so many successions of years, will presume "all to have been solemnly done which were necessary to the perfection of the thing." They will consider the construction of the grant as evidenced by the solemn acts of the constituted authorities of Spain during the Spanish occupancy and dominion of the country, for about twenty-seven years succeeding the grant, as conclusive of its effect and extent.

To shorten the extent of lawful Spanish grants for lands in Louisiana, by bending the words and phrases of the grants from their meaning and lawful effect, according to the Spanish language and Spanish laws, usages, and customs, to subserve the rules of the English common law, is impairing the obligation of the contracts, and violating the faith of the treaty ceding Louisiana to the United States.

GEO. M. BIBB.

WASHINGTON, *March* 13th, 1848.

ERRATA.

Page 3, instead of "*undigested*" read indigested.
Page 6, instead of "*ingunt*" read insunt.
Page 10, instead of "*quosque*" read quousque.
Page 11, instead of "artum" read certum.
Page 20, and second line, strike out "to."
Page 38, line 32, instead of "the" read that.

67 10 — "for-ma"
50 — 10 — "fallit" — falliit (handwritten)